Strange Meetings
Poems by Harold Monro

1879 - 1932

47

For
Ruth Tomalin and Joy Grant

STRANGE MEETINGS
Poems by
HAROLD MONRO

1879 – 1932

A New Selection
edited
with an
Introduction and Notes
by
Dominic Hibberd

Laurel Books

First published in 2003
by Laurel Books
282 The Common Holt Wiltshire BA14 6QJ

Printed by
Antony Rowe Ltd
Bumpers Farm Chippenham Wiltshire SN14 6LH

A CIP record for this book is available from the British Library

ISBN 1-873390-05-X

Cover designed by Jane Stephenson Ingram
based on a drawing of Harold Monro by E. McKnight Kauffer

CONTENTS

from *Real Property* (1922)

from *The Earth for Sale* (1928)

INTRODUCTION

Harold Monro's poetry is extraordinary and impressive. It deserves to be much more widely known. His work was rightly described by his friend and contemporary, Edward Thomas, as 'always intensely interesting'. It resists easy classification. Ezra Pound regarded Monro as a traditionalist, Henry Newbolt described him as a born revolutionary. T.S. Eliot said his poetry was unique to itself, making comparisons with other poets irrelevant. Monro's dogged refusal to join any school or movement may be one reason why he has been neglected for so long, yet he was a central figure, living and working at the heart of early twentieth-century poetry.

Monro is a poet of mysterious encounters with the familiar and the unknown, half-recognitions in the rooms and passageways of the mind, glimpses of hell and 'oracles of Paradise'. Sometimes he seems to echo Eliot, Wilfred Owen, D.H. Lawrence and others among the many writers he knew, but if there are echoes they usually go the other way: Monro was there first. The success of his labours on behalf of other people's poetry has tended to obscure the value of his own, but he wanted above all to be remembered as a poet in his own right.

Eliot said in his introduction to the *Collected Poems* (1933) that Monro's poetry as a whole was 'more nearly the real right thing than any of the poetry of a somewhat older generation than mine except Mr Yeats's'. While it is true that most of the poets in that generation were of little interest to Eliot, he made his judgement after a careful re-reading of Monro's poems. The best of them are the real right thing—and they are of considerable historical interest, reflecting the enormous changes that English poetry went through in the first three turbulent decades of the last century.

One or two of the poems, anthology pieces about animals and the countryside, are still relatively familiar. However, Eliot thought they were far from typical: for him, Monro's central concern had been 'the spectres and the "bad dreams" which live inside the skull, in the ceaseless question and answer of the tortured mind, or the unspoken question and answer between two human beings'. By contrast, Pound described Monro as a poet who had brooded over the collapse of an era.

These very different comments by Eliot and Pound suggest that Monro is best approached through contraries. In some poems he is almost a Modernist, in others almost a Georgian, although he belonged to neither camp. He was fascinated by new ideas and poetry, but a portrait of Keats always hung above his desk. He wrote a lot about rural subjects, was a prodigious walker and always had a country cottage as a retreat for thinking and writing, yet, as Eliot pointed out, he was not a nature poet: in fact he was an inveterate, albeit conscience-ridden town-dweller, 'Remembering as one must all day, / Under the pavement the live earth aches'. He wrote with disarming honesty and courage—but also with the reticence that both Eliot and Owen commented on—about his own inner world, a locked room in a house doomed to decay. He also wrote about public issues, often passionately. He was a keen Utopian, but a practical one, a publisher, editor and bookseller. He was a victim of hope—and of terrible, crushing despair.

Monro's poems record the new century's move from late Romanticism and Victorian orthodoxies to the surge of optimism in the years before the First World War, and through the miseries of that war to the foreboding of the nineteen-twenties. At his most positive, he believed that humanity could perfect itself by achieving a right relationship with the earth, and he dreamed of what he called 'the beautiful Future', the coming dawn. 'Paradise', 'freedom' and 'earth' are key words in his poems. But another key element is frequent, baffled questioning.

When the future arrived in 1914, it was not the glorious sunrise he had looked for. Foreseeing from the start what was going to happen to youth and hope, he was the first of the 'war poets', the founder of what is now thought of as the typical poetry of 1914-18. The most likely relationship with the earth now would be the merging of a soldier's body into clay:

You clutch and claim with passionate grasp of your fingers
The dip of earth in which your body lingers . . .

The many other strange meetings in the poems, between human and earth or between human and human, are inconclusive. Recognition and intimacy are always just out of reach. Monro's late work is often about distance, separation and the 'locked door' of solitude and death—and the earth itself in the end is 'covered with large auction boards', ready for sale to industry, housing and what we would now call eco-tourism. His final prophecies of a ruined world grew from a life of high ambition and bitter disappointment. Even so, his dedication to poetry did not falter, despite all the pain it had cost him. He never gave up.

* * *

Harold Edward Monro was born in 1879 into a prosperous, upper middle class family. While he was still a child, his father and elder brother died from tuberculosis, and then or later he caught the disease himself, although it was not diagnosed until just before it killed him in 1932. One of its symptoms may have been the chronic intestinal pains he complains of in his diaries; another his extreme variations of mood, from visionary fervour to intense pessimism, made worse by fear of death and an inherited weakness for alcohol.

His poetic ambitions took shape while he was a schoolboy at Radley, and they were encouraged at Cambridge by a fellow student and aspiring poet, Maurice Browne. It was an exciting time to be young, at the start of a new century. The two undergraduates convinced themselves that they were at the beginning of a post-Darwinian age, in which humanity would evolve towards paradise on earth without any need for religion—and poets would be the heralds of the dawn. Monro had inherited just enough money to live on, so he gave up plans to become a lawyer and went to Ireland to write poetry in rural seclusion. Unable to admit to himself that he and his friend were in love with each other, he made the bond as close as propriety allowed by marrying Browne's sister, Dorothy. It was not a wise match: Dorothy, a former hockey international, had no taste for seclusion and not much for poetry.

The Ireland poems, mostly pastiche Keats, were published in 1906, by which time the Monros had returned to England. Browne was burning with excitement again, having read H.G. Wells's *A Modern Utopia*, with its vision of an ideal society governed by an order of voluntary 'Samurai'. He persuaded Monro to join him in recruiting would-be Samurai and starting a Samurai Press to publicise the cause. The Press inevitably foundered, but not before it had produced thirty little volumes, including Monro's *Judas*, a long poem about capitalism and failed ideals, and two collections of bleak verse-dramas about peasant life by the Northumberland poet, Wilfrid Gibson. Sent Monro's *Poems* (1906) by Browne, Gibson said they seemed too 'poetical': he himself had started by writing 'confectionery', but he now preferred 'bread-and-cheese'. That comment could be seen as the start of what has been called 'the Georgian revolt', the first example of one future Georgian poet advising another to modernise his style. Monro cannot really be categorised as a Georgian—even though he coined the term and was to publish and appear in all five volumes of Edward Marsh's famous anthology—but Gibson's criticism struck home.

The collapse of the short-lived Samurai order in early 1908 coincided with the collapse of Monro's marriage. He decided to make a fresh start by walking from Paris to Milan, a 'pilgrimage' from winter to spring, northern respectability to southern freedom. His life and work changed radically from that moment. He stayed in communes of free-thinking idealists—sun-worshippers, socialists, anarchists, vegetarians, followers of every new-age creed. In Zurich he became one of the first poets to undergo psychoanalysis (an experience that seems to have shown him he was predominantly homosexual), and during the next few years he learned much—probably more than any other British writer of the period—about advanced ideas and alternative lifestyles. He divided his time between an ascetic commune near Ascona and a romantic medieval tower in Florence, and it was in Florence that he met the companion he was longing for, an eighteen-year-old Irish-Italian named Arundel del Re, a tall, dark, dreamy youth with a passion for poetry. In the autumn of 1911 the two arrived in London, determined to hasten the birth of the new world by bringing together the poets of the future.

Monro's second collection of poems, *Before Dawn (Poems and Impressions)* (1911), was in effect his manifesto. The 'Impressions' are mostly short, satirical portraits of businessmen, gluttons, priests and other offenders against the ideals he had committed himself to. These poems had been started in Florence immediately after the long walk, and their attempt at a 'bread-and-cheese' style, together with their title (at that time 'modern' poetry was often referred to as 'Impressionist'), mark the beginning of his escape from nineteenth-century conventions. Other, much longer poems in *Before Dawn* set out the values of the beautiful Future. The book opens with 'Two Visions', revealing humanity first in its current guise, hideous, still ape-like, and then in its evolved splendour as 'the Titan of the dawn'. Other poems describe the woman of the future, gazing fearlessly at the sunrise; Christ returning to build a socialist paradise; King Arthur returning to rally the Samurai; Don Juan rejoicing in hell; and an abbot explaining that God is dead. 'The Virgin', a dramatic monologue illustrating the need for sexual fulfilment, is one of the first studies of its kind in English poetry, written some years before D.H. Lawrence took up the theme.

Monro had clearly been soaking himself in Nietzsche, Wells, Edward Carpenter, Swinburne and other prophets. Some reviewers were worried by his modernity; others welcomed his assault on Victorian repression and Romantic *ennui*. Edward Thomas said that if one were to choose half-a-dozen books to show a Martian what modern poetry was like, *Before Dawn* would be one of them. C. K. Ogden said that 'Mr Monro must be listened to'. But Monro himself was unsatisfied, aware that he knew 'too much to go on writing the old sort of stuff and too little to write any new,' as he told Browne. Despite Gibson's advice, he had not fully understood that what the poetry of the future needed above all was a new language. New ideas, though *Before Dawn* was full of them, were not enough.

Monro started his campaign in London by founding a periodical which survives to this day, *The Poetry Review*. The *Review's* monthly numbers throughout 1912 remain an indispensable record of the development of English—and French and American—poetry in a crucial year. He befriended many poets, but his strenuous efforts to bring them together were rewarded, much to his disappointment, with the schism between the group soon to be known as 'Georgians', led by Rupert Brooke, and a noisy minority faction, now known as 'Modernists', led by Ezra Pound.

Monro kept going, heartened by lively public interest in what Brooke called 'the New Poetry', and at the end of 1912 he took an old house, 35 Devonshire (now Boswell) Street, in a run-down part of Bloomsbury to be a centre for poets, a 'Poetry House' where they could read and sell their work, discuss it with each other and their readers and even rent bedrooms.[1] For the next twenty years the Poetry Bookshop was to be the most famous meeting-place for poets in the English-speaking world. Monro lost his first periodical (the *Review's* sponsor, the Poetry Society, had decided he was

[1] At almost exactly the same time, Maurice Browne, now married and in the USA, opened another Samurai-inspired enterprise, the Little Theatre in Chicago, which was to make an important contribution to American drama.

much too progressive to be a suitable editor), but he started another, *Poetry and Drama*, and he began publishing books, the first of which—probably in origin his own idea—was *Georgian Poetry 1911–1912*, an anthology of the best work of the new reign, edited by Edward Marsh with advice from Brooke.

By 1913 Monro was well established in literary London. He was always ready to support new talent: many young poets began their careers and met their fellow poets with his help. Customers at the shop and guests at his frequent parties saw a tall, lean, almost military figure, dark-haired, dark-eyed and intensely serious, with a slow, kindly smile. The smile never quite contradicted the melancholy of the eyes. Monro's closest friends were devoted to him, and evenings with them were often hilarious, but he was not a happy man. He blamed himself for neglecting his own writing, believing that his marriage and now his campaigning for poetry were preventing him from reaching the poetic heights he had hoped for. He was trying to write an epic for the age, 'The Death of Jehovah', a vast survey of the rise and fall of religion, but it seemed—and was—a hopeless project. He felt trapped.

On 14 March 1913, his thirty-fourth birthday, he was guest of honour at a Poets' Club dinner, where a beautiful young idealist and suffragette, Alida Klemantaski, had been asked to read from his poems. She fell in love with him, soon becoming the Bookshop's keenest helper, edging out Arundel del Re. Monro loved her, too, and sometimes they slept together, but he was apprehensive, remembering his disastrous relationship with Dorothy. He tried to warn Alida, but she would not listen.

Despite worries about his personal life, Monro produced some of his most successful poems during his first few years in London. Having been isolated as a writer before 1912, he was now at the centre of the 'New Poetry' and his work underwent a startling change. The language—spare, colloquial, fantastic—of the mysterious dialogue, 'Overheard on a Saltmarsh', one of his most well-known works, is unlike anything he had written before. The poem was probably based on a tempestuous affair between del Re and an actress; its strong erotic undertones emerge when it is read aloud, and it can still delight an audience. Monro was an exceptionally good reader of verse, and he liked to read his poems aloud to Alida or some other critical listener before publication, checking for faults. Poetry should be heard: so he resisted the Modernist inclination to write 'for the study'. Nevertheless, he saw the importance of Modernist ideas. 'London Interior' and several other 1912 poems reflect the principles of 'Impressionism' recently laid down by T.E. Hulme, soon to be reformulated by Pound and F.S. Flint as 'Imagism': direct treatment of the object, and freedom from abstractions, rigid forms, superfluous words and what Pound called 'emotional slither'.

Monro's connections with Modernism have often been ignored by academics, who sometimes appear to know little about him except the endlessly repeated accusation that he refused to publish Eliot and Thomas. He did undoubtedly decide against first books by both poets, probably because he thought they would not sell in wartime (the Bookshop's losses had to be made up from his own pocket), but the old story about his dismissing 'The Love Song of J. Alfred Prufrock' as nonsense is not reliable.[2] What is certain is that he admired Eliot's poem when it was published, and he gave what may well have been the first public reading of it, as he did later of *The Waste Land*. Eliot and Flint were among his most loyal friends.

Monro contributed to the birth of Imagism and became one of its earliest, most appreciative critics. He published Pound's anthology, *Des Imagistes* (1914), and might have appeared in it himself if he had been willing to commit his periodical to the cause. Four of his poems did appear in Pound's *Catholic Anthology 1914-1915* (1915), a counterblast to *Georgian Poetry*, alongside 'Prufrock' and four

[2] For the Eliot story and other biographical matters referred to here, see my *Harold Monro: Poet of the New Age* (2001).

other poems by Eliot. But Monro was a democrat, open to all new styles and opinions. Pound scorned him for that, telling him later that 'HELL—you never have had a programme'. Few poets have had higher aims than Monro, but his social idealism was at odds with the Modernist concentration on form and language. Literary theory on its own was of no great interest to him. Sometimes he wrote like the Georgians (though more intelligently, Eliot said in a review), using plain language, traditional forms and often rustic subject-matter. His most popular poem, 'Milk for the Cat', earned respect from all sides and a place in both the *Catholic Anthology* and *Georgian Poetry*. It is still an anthology favourite, but its author wearied of being asked for it again and again, complaining that his less conventional work was always neglected.

When war broke out in 1914, Monro was neither fit nor young enough to be a likely soldier. He volunteered for civilian duties with his motorbike, serving for a while as a part-time special constable. The country was soon awash with patriotic poetry, although none of it seemed any good. In the September *Poetry and Drama* he urged poets to write about the 'plain facts' and 'human psychology' of war. What moved him most was the sight of his young friends deciding to join the army, and he put his feelings into a quartet of poems, 'Youth in Arms'. These poems, and Gibson's 'Breakfast' (October 1914), are the earliest attempts to convey front-line actualities in the Great War, using psychological realism and 'plain facts' taken from newspaper reports. The themes of Monro's four poems—young innocence and its exploitation by 'old men', actual experience, extreme physical and mental strain, the beauty and death of youth—were to be developed later by Siegfried Sassoon and other soldiers who could write from experience, and above all by Owen, who read 'Youth in Arms' in 1915.

At first the war brought some benefits for Monro. He had to give up *Poetry and Drama*, redirecting the Bookshop's publishing efforts towards rhyme sheets, which sold in tens of thousands over the years, and 'chapbooks', little paperbacks of carefully-chosen verse. 1914–16 chapbooks included first books by Richard Aldington, Robert Graves and Charlotte Mew, and Monro's third collection, *Children of Love* (December 1914). In 1915, freed from the incessant labour of editing a periodical, he had time for his own poetry. Eliot's opinion that Monro's last work was his best has generally been accepted, but the long poems of 1915–16 have some claim to be seen as his most original and characteristic writing.

Increasingly the news was of death. Monro became one of the first critics to protest at the mythologising of Rupert Brooke, saying that Brooke's death was merely one more example of the war's 'dreary and incomprehensible waste'. The elegy, 'Lament in 1915', records his grief at the loss of Basil Watt, a witty, handsome actor and sportsman who had lived at the Bookshop as Monro's secretary and probably lover in 1914. In the 'Lament', as elsewhere in Monro's mature work, strong feeling takes his style close to the border between verse and prose.

> Some men are killed . . . not you. Be you as you were.
> And yet—Somehow it's dark down all the stair.
> I'm standing at the door. You are not there.

Nineteenth-century diction is now left far behind, and an individual voice speaks from the heart in plain words.

Monro's convictions prevented him from turning to the standard wartime consolations, that soldiers were dying in a noble cause and earning themselves places in heaven. Instead, he sought comfort in the countryside, even though he knew he did not belong there. The slow life of trees seemed to offer a kind of immortality on earth: in 'Trees' he records a strange spiritual exercise, an attempt to enter the trees' dimension, where perhaps some men might live beyond the death of the body. The attempt fails, but he remained a lover of trees all his life, their beauty inspiring some of his most rhapsodic writing.

'Be true to the earth', Nietzsche had urged the people of the dawn. Monro's theme of humanity and earth is put into domestic terms in the 1915-16 sonnet-sequence, 'Week-end', a celebration of escapes to the country with Alida. Some readers regard 'Week-end' as his most appealing poem; others are embarrassed by the apparent whimsicality of its animated pots and kettles. Its seriousness tends to be overlooked. As in 'Trees', he is remembering the teaching of G.E. Moore, a philosopher who had influenced Brooke and many Bloomsbury writers. 'Glad worship of the visible world and incurable belief in the beauty of material things' was, according to Moore, enough for a full and purposeful life. Monro worshipped devoutly. Some of his most memorable poetry is about material things—plants, animals, furniture, houses. But he could never be at peace for long: the forest rejects him, the country cottage has to be left to its resident ghosts on Monday morning—and Alida, 'child of the earth' as he described her, had to become once again, in her own bitter phrase, 'the woman who runs the shop'. The Blake-like 'oracles' and lyrics of the best of the 1915-16 sequences, 'Strange Meetings', are full of puzzlement and questioning. Always searching for faith and meaning, Monro is a religious poet, despite his vigorous disbelief in God.

Monro and Dorothy were granted a decree nisi, the prelude to a divorce, in April 1916, by which time conscription had been introduced. Single men were due to be called up first, so he took the last chance to volunteer and in July became a Second Lieutenant in the Royal Garrison Artillery. Rated unfit for overseas service, he was put on anti-aircraft duties in England. Home service was humiliating, despised by both civilians and front-line soldiers. He hated every moment of it, the discipline, the monotony, the unbearable waste of time. The sunlit near-paradise of 'Week-end' gave way to the dismal scenery of 'Aspidistra Street', his Manchester lodgings in the winter of 1916-17.

Finished with Dorothy at last, he completed 'Coronilla', a memory of her sexual appetite. He wrote more kindly about Alida, but he was not altogether regretful at being away from her, either, with her insistent demands to be his only close companion. She was doomed, he knew, to ever greater disappointment. During the next few years she slowly discovered about his drinking and his many affairs with young men. It was perhaps his drinking as well as his politics that got him into quarrels with his fellow officers, who suspected him of being a pacifist and therefore, in their view, a coward. Mental and physical strain put him in hospital several times. In 1918 he was moved to a desk job in London at the Ministry of Information, where his fluency in French, German and Italian could be put to use, but it was too late. His health and spirits were never to recover from his time in the army.

By the time Monro was demobilised in March 1919, he was on the edge of breakdown. Nevertheless he threw himself into reviving the Bookshop and planning yet another periodical, *The Chapbook*. A new generation of poets, typified by the Sitwells, gathered at his parties in a post-war atmosphere of brittle gaiety. Seriousness was out of fashion. He tried to persuade himself that the aim of poetry should be to entertain, but he knew that was a betrayal of his earlier beliefs. The war had destroyed his ideals and killed many poets, including some of his dearest friends. The poets who survived were leaving him behind, often showing little gratitude for the help he had given them. His own work seemed out of date again. Echoing his remark about 'the old sort of stuff' in 1911, he told Marsh that his mind was 'in a state of upheaval and transition, so that I can't polish the old things, nor make myself at home in the new phase'.

The Bookshop published the fourth volume of *Georgian Poetry* in November 1919. Monro had been doubtful, knowing that Marsh's taste had become ever more conservative since Brooke's death, but the anthology was the shop's most celebrated title and the risk had to be taken. The new book sold well, but it was derided by reviewers. Some of Monro's own lyrics came in for ridicule. He had often been described as a Georgian, and the shop, equally inaccurately, had often been regarded as a Georgian headquarters. Miserably hurt, he now tried to distance himself, his enterprises and above all his own poetry from everything 'Georgian'. His *Some Contemporary Poets* (1920), the only book of criticism he ever wrote, is a unique survey of poetry in the period immediately before *The Waste Land*, but its scathing comments on most of the Georgians caused astonishment and yet more ridicule. It was a bad start to the decade, made worse by his marrying Alida in March 1920, a tormenting surrender to respectability.

The failure of the Georgian movement left the way open for Modernism. Monro had always been sympathetic, despite his differences with Pound, and in the post-war world he was sure that Eliot represented the best hope for the poetry of the future. He gave the new leader all the help he could, publishing him in the *Chapbook* and advising on the form of Eliot's own periodical, *The Criterion*. Eliot regarded him as a member of his editorial 'inner circle', and his magazine's supporters, the *Criterion* Club, met regularly at the Bookshop. Several of Monro's poems seem to be echoed in *The Waste Land*. One of the many curious notes he made about London characters—'Albert's story:— woman in pub . . . False teeth'— suggests that he provided material for the Cockney monologue in Eliot's poem. He was collecting incidents and scraps of conversation for possible use in plays and short stories. Eliot could have found no better informant about nightlife in the 'unreal city'. The two men often met, sharing a fondness for cats and whisky as well as poetry.

Monro's fifth collection, *Real Property*, came out in March 1922, only months before *The Waste Land*. Like Eliot, he presented his new poems as fragments. He had been hoping since 1916 to write a long series on true 'real property', humanity's few, inalienable possessions—the earth, heredity, consciousness, the 'silent pool' of the unconscious, memory, sexuality, the longing for perfection, and so on. It was an ambitious, Jungian project, but in the end only twelve sections were completed. These were no doubt among the poems that Eliot had in mind when he said that Monro had written about 'the ceaseless question and answer of the tortured mind'. He recognised Monro as in some ways a kindred spirit: in places the *Real Property* 'fragments' come close to his own concerns and methods.

> . . . one will rise and sadly shake his head;
> Another will but comb and comb her hair,
> While some will move untiringly about
> Through all the rooms, for ever in and out,
> Or up and down the stair . . .

Conrad Aiken could have been thinking of *Real Property*, too, when he described Monro's 'kinky' poetry as having 'a kind of angry desperation': 'in its dogged insistence on the literal truth, nothing less, and every inch of it, it tangled itself in the contingent, got helplessly in its own way, and suddenly came to an end exhausted.'[3] Aiken was right that many of the poems do end inconclusively, as though the energy has suddenly gone out of them. The ceaseless questions were unanswerable, even though Monro had spent years researching for 'The Death of Jehovah', investigating religion in its many forms. He was too serious-minded and too honest to abandon fact and reason or be content with superficialities, yet he could not bear the thought that life might be meaningless.

Nevertheless, although some of his poems end in bafflement, others are confident, finely shaped and polished. The form of 'Man Carrying Bale', for example, one of the poems in a separate lyric section of *Real Property*, is precisely suited to content, the lines and line breaks mirroring the subject's movements. Some of Monro's most positive concerns—sunlight, time, archetypes, the beauty of labour and masculine strength, the mutuality of mind, body and earth—are brought compactly together.

He was defensive about the lyrics in *Real Property*, saying in his introduction that they were 'tainted with slight *Georgian* affectations', but he knew they were worth publishing. One of

---

[3] Conrad Aiken, *Ushant* (1952), p.258.

them, 'Unknown Country', which he thought 'almost too *Georgian'* even for *Georgian Poetry,* actually expresses a thoroughly un-Georgian sense of alienation. Rustic people, like the trees, do not accept him. Even the youths belong to another world.

> Sun-freckled lads, who at the dusk of day
> Stroll through the village with a scent of hay
> Clinging about you from the windy hill,
> Why do you keep your secret from me still?
> You loiter at the corner of the street . . .

Lads loitering on London streets might be there to be picked up, but the country was different. Frustrated desire—for love, cleanliness, strength, innocence, beauty—runs all through Monro's poetry. His own tormented sexuality was at the heart of his difficulties. He was never able to talk or write about it openly, despite his honesty and literalness, and all his reading in the latest psychology and philosophy could not solve the problem for him. He loved the earth but was a stranger on it.

Several old dreams ended in the six-year gap between *Real Property* and Monro's last collection, *The Earth for Sale* (1928). Del Re got married, the *Chapbook* failed, and Monro finally gave up trying to write a modern epic. The lease on 35 Devonshire Street ran out in 1926. It was painful to leave the old house—'We were not wrong, believing that it cared'—but Monro took larger premises at 38 Great Russell Street, opposite the British Museum, and for a moment things looked hopeful. Then his mother died, leaving him far less money than he had always counted on, and he had to make drastic economies. The shop was moved to a rear extension, entered from Willoughby Street at the side: thus hidden away, it made increasing losses. Customers who found the door were often deterred from further visits by the proprietor's gloomy, sometimes drunken presence.

Most of the poems in *The Earth for Sale* are about personal loss and isolation. There was almost nothing to cling to, except Alida's loyalty, and even that was best thought of at a distance. He made poetry out of the things he had fought against: emptiness, silence, the lack of answers. In his early days he had often written at excessive length, but the late poems, and their lines and words, tend to be short.

> I cannot find a way
> Through love and through;
> I cannot reach beyond
> Body, to you.

Brevity and reticence became integral to the best of his writing. There could be no way out of the locked room ('There never is,' Eliot said grimly). Sometimes nature—sunlight, the call of a ring-dove, the promise of spring—might still hint at paradise, but Monro's pessimism was about the planet's future as well as his own. He was appalled at the likely results of post-war building and over-population, imagining a final 'strange meeting' when people would face each other at last in the world they had overwhelmed and destroyed.

> How shall we meet that moment when we know
> There is no room to grow;
> We, conscious, and with lonely startled eyes
> Glaring upon ourselves, and with no Lord
> To pray to: judged, without appeal,
> What shall we feel?

The 'beautiful Future' was now going to be an automated paradise, where millions would be casually slaughtered in war games and tourists would gawp at 'the last, last, Nature Poet'.

In the end Monro took refuge in the 'bitter sanctuary' of alcohol, writing one of his finest poems about it.

> He cannot wake himself; he may not slumber;
> While on the long white wall across the road
> Drives the thin outline of a dwindling hearse . . .

He died in 1932. Three years later, Alida had to close the Poetry Bookshop.

*   *   *

One of Alida's first tasks after her husband's death was to arrange for his poems to be published. She made the selection herself, inviting Flint and Eliot to write, respectively, biographical and critical introductions. The *Collected Poems* came out in 1933. There had already been a much shorter selection in 1927, edited by Humbert Wolfe for the Augustan Books of English Poetry series. Alida compiled another short selection, *The Silent Pool and Other Poems*, in 1942. The *Collected Poems* were reissued in 1970 with an invaluable preface by Ruth Tomalin.

In compiling the present selection I have tried to choose poems that would represent not only Monro's best work but also his development from *Before Dawn* onwards. Four poems from *Before Dawn* are reprinted here for the first time. All the other poems are in *Collected Poems*, and all but four of them were included in one or other of the six collections that appeared in Monro's lifetime. I have almost always followed the 1933 text, which usually reproduces the originals as they first appeared in book form. In a very few cases, I have reverted to the punctuation of earlier texts, where it seems a clear improvement. Monro's syntax can sometimes seem odd, occasionally downright wrong, but he was a careful proof reader and I have refrained from making alterations, except for correcting a few typographical errors. The poems are arranged in roughly chronological order, although it is impossible to date all of them precisely. Dates of composition and first publication, where I have been able to discover them, and other factual information will be found in the notes.

Dominic Hibberd

IMPRESSIONS

XI

His hand is broad and flat, of savage power
His will, his voice sonorous: he controls
A thousand engines by his master-wit.
A million men he slowly hour by hour
Murders, first drawing out their weary souls,
Then tearing up their bodies bit by bit.

Who would suspect this man of simple ways,
Unstudious occupations, plain attire—
Clad usually in sanctimonious black,
Of harrowing the consecrated days
With torture of the hammer and the fire,
More slow, more fierce than ancient screw or rack?

I see him at his desk—he looms, a dim
Smoke-wreathèd figure; in the background tower
The chimneys, loud and wild the engines roar:
Gold out of every current flows to him;
Far into foreign lands his magic power
Extends in theft and usury and war.

A time was once when love in him awoke:
Toward his wife he gentle is and fair,
To his own children always good and mild;
Yet he to-day has schemed a master-stroke,
Driving a thousand women to despair,
And murdering many an unsuspecting child.

O mothers, mothers, weep no more! This blind
Black power shall not for ever own the earth:
Behold! a light of promise unwithdrawn
Glimmers and gathers in the sky behind
The smoke and roar. Make ready with your mirth:
You shall go laughing forth into the dawn.

X

He meditates in silence all the day,
Reclining in an atmosphere of dreams:
Meanwhile the bravest moments slip away,
And life is wasted in its crystal streams.

Out of his lips the smoke curls dreamily
Upward, and wreathes about his careless hair;
If you may speak by chance, still silent, he
But gazes at you with a vacant stare.

Thus dwelling in a world where shadows seem
Reality, what succour shall he give?
What value may be set upon his dream,
Who has not learnt, and cannot learn—to live?

Though he may prate of Purpose and of Will,
Propounding many schemes with perfect art,
I know he nothing, nothing shall fulfil—
Because he lacks a true and valiant heart.

VIII

He moves in blood; from his distorted face
It trickles down his garments; on each hand
Is gore and filth: the atmosphere is red
And heavy with the stench that fills the place,
Where he ten loathsome hours a day must stand
Slaughtering that the million may be fed.

His eyes are barren of the natural fire,
From contemplating everlasting pain;
He whistles softly while the soft blood drips.
But, oh, the sudden spasm of desire,
When afterwards he raises once again
The cup of hot oblivion to his lips!

Long since he has forgotten how the light
Shines on his native meadows—mid obscure
Fog-haunted slums his wife and children move:
When he approaches at the fall of night
How may she greet him who can scarce endure
The stench he brings?—They have forgotten love.

Bones, purple skin, dirt, slime and steaming blood,
Entrails, and bits of flesh lie on the ground;
He laughs to see the heavy carcass roll
Dead under the relentless hammer's thud:
High above all a moaning lowing sound
Makes music unto his immortal soul.

I

At sunrise, on the lonely way,
He looms against the fiery sky,
As, to the labour of the day,
I watch him eagerly go by.

His scythe, upon his shoulder borne,
Points weirdly to the gathering light:
His is the symbol of the Morn
Emerging from unconscious night.

And unto him the sacred field
Gives bread to sanctify the feast;
His is the honour of the yield:
We are the supplicants, he the priest.

1908

GO NOW, BELOVED

Go now, belovèd! I too desire it thus.
Go swiftly! but you cannot break the chain.
Fate hath the bitter lordship over us:
        Go now—in vain!

When you are in his arms at dead of night,
Safe in the darkness, though you cannot see,
Sudden shall flash upon your inward sight
        The form of me.

My image will be present in the air:
Though you may strive your weariest to be true,
I, where the sunrays on the carpet flare,
        Shall rise for you.

When you and he together in the spring
At sunset by your open doorway stand,
You shall grow faint, too much remembering
        My voice and hand.

When he shall bring you roses, this last hour
Shall snatch their beauty from you like a thief;
For there shall be remembrance in each flower,
        Stem, thorn and leaf.

Slow year by year I shall become more true,
Until I never leave you day nor night;
Shall faithfully take my station between you
        And all delight.

When he shall pass his fingers through your hair,
However gentle you may be and fond,
Your gaze shall not meet his—your eyes will stare
        At me beyond.

Nor will your agony for me be told,
And peacefully put aside when you must die:
Though all remembrance of your youth grow cold—
       Yet will not I.

I will so haunt you to the verge of death,
That when, in bitterness of spirit, he
Shall lean across you, you with your last breath
       Shall call for me.

Go now, belovèd—but remember, past
The limits of terrestrial love or hate,
I, at the portal of the unknown vast,
       Shall, silent, wait.

1908–10

TWO VISIONS

Two visions came to me. At drear midnight,
    When first I laid my weary head adown,
The chamber filled with chasms on my sight,

And the wide darkness gathered in a frown;
    And I, who had dreamed wonders through the long
Sweet daylight of that last enduring crown

Humanity, the subtle and the strong,
    Should wear as in fulfilment on his brow,
Was haunted by the phantoms that belong

To deepest living Hell. From high to low
    The sultry room was gradually filled
As with vague matter, that began to flow

Into some form, irresolutely willed,
    And palpitating while it gathered shape,
Floated, then sank and groaned; rose, chattered and
                                                    trilled;

Broke in stark faces, mouths and eyes agape;
    Then shrank again and indolently slept;
Then sprang with guttural noises of the ape;

Then drifted, formless, out of sight and wept:
    True to no cause, yet swift in all deceit,
When slumber almost held me, slowly crept

Round the low wainscot, and in violent heat,
    Roared at me, crimson suddenly; then leant
Backward to shake with laughter. I could meet

No steadfast gaze of eyes, although intent
    To find and, staring, hold them; and I heard
No utterance resolute or consequent.

For if some red mouth formed to speak some word,
    It melted ere the word was spoken, and
That hopeless laughter of derision stirred

The wake of all attempt. Or if some hand
    Shot pointing up translucent as a flame,
'Twas quenched before it ever could command.

All things began, but unto nothing came.
    No purpose lingered: none was ever clear.
Once only something like a cry of shame

Brake—like thin smoke to waste and disappear.
    The fiercest impulse ended but in vain,
And sudden laughter dimmed the eyes of fear:

Mirth made it shriek, but scarcely ever, pain.
    Thus all the night it thwarted my repose,
Vanishing for a moment; then again

Appearing mid an agony of throes,
    Like sap in spring miraculously rife,
But drifting as a leaf in autumn goes;

Fierce like a wild beast rushing to the strife,
    But fading, fading pitifully away.
Oh Man! Beloved Humanity! O Life!—

I yearned for the beginning of the day,
    And, when the first faint streak appeared between
The low long clouds like mounds of ashes grey,

Rose swiftly from my hateful couch to lean
    Toward the rising sun upon the sea.
Then, while a cool breath floated from the green,

That other vision was revealed to me.
    Far in a faintly golden mist he stood:
The Titan of the dawn—Humanity.

I was not wanton till you did not come.
Whoever you may be, hear me at last!
Faintly, I do implore you for your hands:
I grope to find them. Stay! I have become
So humble now, that meekly I will follow
Whatever way you lead me through the world.
I have no habitation of my own.
Unsacred is my room, mine images
Unconsecrated, and my lonely bed
Haunted with memories of the wakeful night
All void of love, and of the barren dawn.
It is so weary to begin the days,
To stir, wake, wonder, rise, and breathe again:
O how much longer must I tolerate
The flowerless repetition of the hours,
And little occupations without cause?
Love! Love! I want to lay my body out,
To be all covered over, to receive;
I want to hold, and fasten, and be held:
I hunger; I am starved. . . . And I have thought
Sometimes men gazed upon me half in fear,
As though they guessed my hunger. Gracious God!
I am not vile: I only would obey
Thy law, as thine own stars obey—they rush
Love-swift together, and a million suns
Proceed from that embrace. The stars! Indeed
The filthy worm that feeds upon the corpse
Obeys thee also—loves, and is beloved;
Yet I must clasp my cold hands desperately,
Feed on my strained flesh, and my captive soul
Must beat against the black bars. I was born
Through love; I was created by the law
That makes the low worm equal with the stars:
My father held my mother in his arms,
And while she trembled with delight of him,
I was conceived, and holy was the hour—

Colossal as the silences that brood
   Over the deep, he filled the tranquil sky;
Stained round his ankles still with ancient blood,

But with heroic countenance set high;
   And on his noble brow one morning star
Burned with seraphic flame immortally.

His visionary eyes looked out afar
   Beyond the transient semblances of death.
No sound of supplication came to mar

The rhythm of his calmly-taken breath.
   No ripple of a thin or faint delight
Moved round his crimson lips; and underneath

His bright skin aureoled by the rose twilight
   Rolled the vast torrent of majestic thews.
Master of his strong passion, all the might

Of his tremendous form was fair with use.
   He bent beneath the burden of no load;
He lingered not within the dawn to muse;

Joy of the hero in his motion showed:
   He moved the clear ways of the earth along,
And to the daylight of the orient strode.

Beautiful human body cool and strong,
   In the full consciousness of human pride,
With the slow rhythm of a perfect song,

Uniting in the compass of a stride
   The soil of continent and continent!
O symbol of the earth, ensanctified
   With joyfulness of manhood's high intent!

1909

34
31

THE VIRGIN

Arms that have never held me; lips of him
Who should have been for me; hair most beloved,
I would have smoothed so gently; steadfast eyes,
Half-closed, yet gazing at me through the dusk;
And hands—you sympathetic human hands,
I would have everlastingly adored,
To which I have so often tendered mine
Across the gulf, O far, far, far away
Unwilling hands; and voice of him I have dreamed
So often in the evening by the fire,
Whose step I have heard approaching, at the door
Pausing, but never entering: O tall
And well-beloved imaginary form—
I curse you! Is the silence of the night
Not mine, but you must haunt it? Are my dreams
Not mine, but you must fill them? There were days
I had some little beauty for you—Why
Came you not then? What kept you? Now my lips
Are feverish with longing, and mine eyes,
Wanton with expectation. Where are you?
In what moon-haunted garden? By what stream?
Where whisper you your vows? Among what flowers,
(Which bloom though I am barren)? To what maid
Of cream and rose in muslin?—And her hand
Touches you lightly, while you tremble. She
Had waited also; but you came to her.
I would not be revengeful—yet of late
I dream of every maiden I behold,
She may have won you from me. Oh, believe!
None other can have loved you as I would.
So long, so long have I imagined you;
Yea, from my foolish girlhood, every night
Have held you in my arms. Forgive me, love!
You seemed so nearly mine; and every morning

I cried "To-day!" And often in my prayers
When I would try to think of Jesus Christ,
It only seemed as if I thought of you.
Oh, surely I deserved some better fate
Than this black barren destitution. I
Am made of flesh, and I have tingling nerves:
My blood is always hot, and I desire
The touch of gentle hands upon my face
To cool it, as the moonlight cools the earth.
There is no peace. In spring, the turtle doves
Madden me with their crooning, and the trees
Whisper all day together. Everywhere
There is some festival of love. Alas,
Men in all places openly declare
Love is the world, and maidens, with a blush,
Hint beautiful devotion. Know they not
I am a woman—I could too have served?
Sometimes (young matrons look upon me so),
I laugh aloud in everybody's face
Instead of weeping, for I have to choose
Quickly. That sudden laugh without a cause
Has grown into a habitude of late:
Thus people stare at me, and shake their heads
And sign to one another with their eyes.
Then afterwards I always have to go
Alone to drench my pillow with my tears. . . .
You, you, who have not loved me, who have f
Some other consolation in the world,
Who are my cause and complement of woe,
Say, what can be achieved through such as I?
I cannot change the pattern of my soul.
It surely is not evil to desire:
Mothers desire their children, and the priest
Desires his God; the earth desires the sun;
And I lean out in agony for you;
So very long I had expected you:

But I shall die for want of being loved.
Truly it is not just. With my despair
I am a creature so lascivious now,
That no one anywhere is safe. Mine eyes
Wander and rest, and wander and devour.
I meditate on subtle-hearted plans,
And small deceits, and rasping jealousies.
My voice is sour or bitter, and I blush
Suddenly without reason, or I hang
For reassurance on some trivial words
Spoken in jest, or suddenly I feel
Covered with guilty shame, and swift must go
To drench my lonely pillow with my tears.
Or I seek out the mirror, with mine eyes
To gaze in mine own eyes, and smooth my hair,
Or sometimes to adorn it with a rose,
Imagining I may be beautiful.
Indeed, indeed, my hair is very black,
My skin most white—most pallid. . . . O you powers
That guard the destiny of woman, you
Have wronged me somehow: surely you have erred.
What consolation have you left for me?
Indeed I had been worthy of some love:
I cannot keep my thoughts away from that,
That always—for my life is on the leash:
I have not ever yet begun to live.
But after benediction of warm arms,
After delight of consecrative hands,
After firm, hot and sympathetic lips
Pressed hard upon me—afterward my flesh
Had leapt to vigour; my disjointed thoughts
Had followed one another in stern train
Of consequence. My life would have begun:
I should have been beloved. . . . Alas! Oh God!
God! Where has passion led me? To what shame!
I have become a harlot in my thoughts.

I am no fit companion for myself.
I must begin again, must wash my soul,
Accept my fate in silence, and be pure.
There *is* some consolation. Have I not
Neglected my devotion? I must pray.
Will He not help me if I pray to Him?
Are there not many virgins in the world
Who yield their spirits to Him, and so remain
Silent, reflective, beautiful? But I
Rage like a wanton. Though the days be long,
And God seem always absent, though the nights
Be longer; nevertheless I will be pure. . . .
Yet know I many mothers without taint;
Silent, reflective, beautiful are they,
Being beloved—and surely they are pure.
God! God! You are not just, for you yourself
Were known unto a virgin, and your son
Was born, and you had your delight therein.
You are not just, and your Heaven is too far;
I cannot fix my countenance on you:
I have too much devotion for the earth.
You should descend upon me, for I gasp
To hold and to possess some living form.
Alas! My life is dragging from its prime.
My days are bitter with salt tears. Lo, I
Shall pass into the shadow, and the gloom
Will fold me hard about. I shall decay
Slowly like withered flowers. The atmosphere
Will sicken all around me. I shall droop
Towards the tomb, shall stumble, and shall fall.
My body will be covered with rank earth.
My nostrils will be stopped. I shall remain
Alone and unbeloved for evermore.

c 1910

PARADISE

Belovèd, I had given you my soul,
(Which is my body): you and I had dwelt
One year in paradise—when God appeared.
He saw us very simple: we would pass
Whole days in contemplation of some thought
Frail as a white narcissus. We desired
The earth, and found the beauty of the earth
In one another. We had paradise,
And would have dwelt eternally therein,
Had God not, in the likeness of a snake,
Crept in between us, had he not become
Jealous as he is wont. Alas! Alas!
Belovèd, evil are the ways of God.
Let us not fear him, nor with suppliant hands
Ask any mercy from him out of heaven.
He gave us not this dreaming love of ours,
Nor paradise, nor any flower therein:
Nor shall he take them from us. He is God
Sole and elect of all the world outside,
And I had seen him roaming at the dusk
In the semblance of a man, cunning and huge,
Jealously round the gates, before he crept
Between us like a serpent, and declared
He would barter all the gold he holds in heaven
For one frail flower of paradise. Belovèd,
Let us continue children of the earth
Among the simple flowers—tall lilies, pansies,
And white narcissus; for a little care
They fill the night with perfume: and if God
Breaks in upon us by some stratagem,
Let us remain apart with silent eyes,
Not fearing, scarce perceiving, to ourselves
Complete in one another till the end.
The tread of God is murder: if he comes

Pursuing us with vengeance, let us stand
Together, silent still, against some tree,
Whose sacred life we shall be conscious of
Within trunk, boughs and leaves. Thus let us pass,
If need be underneath the foot of God,
Back to the everlasting, out of which
We have, belovèd, this little season dwelt
Together with our flowers in paradise.

1910

OVERHEARD ON A SALTMARSH

Nymph, nymph, what are your beads?
Green glass, goblin. Why do you stare at them?
Give them me.
>   No.
Give them me. Give them me.
>   No.
Then I will howl all night in the reeds,
Lie in the mud and howl for them.

Goblin, why do you love them so?

They are better than stars or water,
Better than voices of winds that sing,
Better than any man's fair daughter,
Your green glass beads on a silver ring.

Hush I stole them out of the moon.

Give me your beads, I desire them.
>   No.
I will howl in a deep lagoon
For your green glass beads, I love them so.
Give them me. Give them.
>   No.

1912

LONDON INTERIOR

Autumn is in the air,
The children are playing everywhere.

One dare not open this old door too wide;
It is so dark inside.
The hall smells of dust;
A narrow squirt of sunlight enters high,
Cold, yellow.
The floor creaks, and I hear a sigh,
Rise in the gloom and die.

Through the hall, far away,
I just can see
The dingy garden with its wall and tree.
A yellow cat is sitting on the wall
Blinking toward the leaves that fall.
And now I hear a woman call
Some child from play.

Then all is still. Time must go
Ticking slow, glooming slow.

The evening will turn grey.
It is sad in London after two.
All, all the afternoon
What can old men, old women do?

It is sad in London when the gloom
Thickens, like wool,
In the corners of the room;
The sky is shot with steel,
Shot with blue.

The bells ring the slow time;
The chairs creak, the hours climb;
The sunlight lays a streak upon the floor.

1912

THE STRANGE COMPANION
(A Fragment)

That strange companion came on shuffling feet,
Passed me, then turned, and touched my arm.

He said (and he was melancholy,
And both of us looked fretfully,
And slowly we advanced together)
He said: "I bring you your inheritance."

I watched his eyes; they were dim.
I doubted him, watched him, doubted him. . .
But, in a ceremonious way,
He said: "You are too grey:
Come, you must be merry for a day."

And I, because my heart was dumb,
Because the life in me was numb,
Cried: "I will come. I *will* come."

So, without another word,
We two jaunted on the street.
I had heard, often heard,
The shuffling of those feet of his,
The shuffle of his feet.

And he muttered in my ear
Such a wheezy jest
As a man may often hear—
Not the worst, not the best
That a man may hear.

Then he murmured in my face
Something that was true.
He said: "I have known this long, long while,
All there is to know of you."
And the light of the lamp cut a strange smile

On his face, and we muttered along the street,
Good enough friends, on the usual beat.

We lived together long, long.
We were always alone, he and I.
We never smiled with each other;
We were like brother and brother,
Dimly accustomed.
                    Can a man know
Why he must live, or whether he should go?

He brought me that joke or two,
And we roared with laughter, for want of a smile,
As every man in the world might do.

He who lies all night in bed
Is a fool, and midnight will crush his head.

When he threw a glass of wine in my face
One night, I hit him, and we parted;
But in a short space
We came back to each other melancholy hearted,
Told our pain,
Swore we would not part again.

One night we turned a table over
The body of some slain fool to cover,
And all the company clapped their hands;
So we spat in their faces,
And travelled away to other lands.

I wish for every man he find
A strange companion so
Completely to his mind
With whom he everywhere may go.

1909–13

HEARTHSTONE

I want nothing but your fireside now.
Friend, you are sitting there alone I know,
And the quiet flames are licking up the soot,
Or crackling out of some enormous root:
All the logs on your hearth are four feet long.
Everything in your room is wide and strong
According to the breed of your hard thought.
Now you are leaning forward; you have caught
That great dog by his paw and are holding it,
And he looks sidelong at you, stretching a bit,
Drowsing with open eyes, huge, warm and wide,
The full hearth-length on his slow-breathing side.
Your book has dropped unnoticed: you have read
So long you cannot send your brain to bed.
The low quiet room and all its things are caught
And linger in the meshes of your thought.
(Some people think they know time cannot pause.)
Your eyes are closing now though not because
Of sleep. You are searching something with your brain;
You have let the old dog's paw drop down again. . . .
Now suddenly you hum a little catch,
And pick up the book. The wind rattles the latch;
There's a patter of light cool rain and the curtain shakes;
The silly dog growls, moves, and almost wakes.
The kettle near the fire one moment hums.
Then a long peace upon the whole room comes.
So the sweet evening will draw to its bedtime end.
I want nothing now but your fireside, friend.

c 1914

SUBURB

Dull and hard the low wind creaks
Among the rustling pampas plumes.
Drearily the year consumes
Its fifty-two insipid weeks.

Most of the grey-green meadow land
Was sold in parsimonious lots;
The dingy houses stand
Pressed by some stout contractor's hand
Tightly together in their plots.

Through builded banks the sullen river
Gropes, where its houses crouch and shiver.
Over the bridge the tyrant train
Shrieks, and emerges on the plain.

In all the better gardens you may pass,
(Product of many careful Saturdays),
Large red geraniums and tall pampas grass
Adorn the plots and mark the gravelled ways.

Sometimes in the background may be seen
A private summer-house in white or green.
Here on warm nights the daughter brings
Her vacillating clerk,
To talk of small exciting things
And touch his fingers through the dark.

He, in the uncomfortable breach
Between her trilling laughters,
Promises, in halting speech,
Hopeless immense Hereafters.

She trembles like the pampas plumes.
Her strained lips haggle. He assumes
The serious quest. . . .

Now as the train is whistling past
He takes her in his arms at last.

It's done. She blushes at his side
Across the lawn—a bride, a bride.

The stout contractor will design,
The lazy labourers will prepare,
Another villa on the line;
In the little garden-square
Pampas grass will rustle there.

c 1914

MILK FOR THE CAT

When the tea is brought at five o'clock,
And all the neat curtains are drawn with care,
The little black cat with bright green eyes
Is suddenly purring there.

At first she pretends, having nothing to do,
She has come in merely to blink by the grate,
But, though tea may be late or the milk may be sour,
She is never late.

And presently her agate eyes
Take a soft large milky haze,
And her independent casual glance
Becomes a stiff hard gaze.

Then she stamps her claws or lifts her ears
Or twists her tail and begins to stir,
Till suddenly all her lithe body becomes
One breathing trembling purr.

The children eat and wriggle and laugh;
The two old ladies stroke their silk:
But the cat is grown small and thin with desire,
Transformed to a creeping lust for milk.

The white saucer like some full moon descends
At last from the clouds of the table above;
She sighs and dreams and thrills and glows,
Transfigured with love.

She nestles over the shining rim,
Buries her chin in the creamy sea;
Her tail hangs loose; each drowsy paw
Is doubled under each bending knee.

A long dim ecstasy holds her life;
Her world is an infinite shapeless white,
Till her tongue has curled the last holy drop,
Then she sinks back into the night,

Draws and dips her body to heap
Her sleepy nerves in the great arm-chair,
Lies defeated and buried deep
Three or four hours unconscious there.

c 1914

YOUTH IN ARMS

I

Happy boy, happy boy,
David the immortal willed,
Youth a thousand thousand times
Slain, but not once killed,
Swaggering again to-day
In the old contemptuous way;

Leaning backward from your thigh
Up against the tinselled bar—
Dust and ashes! is it you?
Laughing, boasting, there you are!
First we hardly recognised you
In your modern avatar.

Soldier, rifle, brown khaki—
Is your blood as happy so?
Where's your sling, or painted shield,
Helmet, pike, or bow?
Well, you're going to the wars—
That is all you need to know.

Greybeards plotted. They were sad.
Death was in their wrinkled eyes.
At their tables, with their maps
Plans and calculations, wise
They all seemed; for well they knew
How ungrudgingly Youth dies.

At their green official baize
They debated all the night
Plans for your adventurous days
Which you followed with delight,
Youth in all your wanderings,
David of a thousand slings.

II

SOLDIER

Are you going? To-night we must all hear your laughter;
We shall need to remember it in the quiet days after.
Lift your rough hands, grained like unpolished oak.
Drink, call, lean forward, tell us some happy joke.
Let us know every whim of your brain and innocent soul.
Your speech is let loose; your great loafing words roll
Like hill-waters. But every syllable said
Brings you nearer the time you'll be found lying dead
In a ditch, or rolled stiff on the stones of a plain.
(Thought! Thought go back into your kennel again:
Hound, back!) Drink your glass, happy soldier, to-night.
Death is quick; you will laugh as you march to the fight.
We are wrong. Dreaming ever, we falter and pause:
You go forward unharmed without Why or Because.
Spring does not question. The war is like rain;
You will fall in the field like a flower without pain;
And who shall have noticed one sweet flower that dies?
The rain comes; the leaves open, and other flowers rise.
The old clock tolls. Now all our words are said.
We drift apart and wander away to bed.
We dream of War. *Your* closing eyelids keep
Quiet watch upon your heavy dreamless sleep.
You do not wonder if you shall, nor why,
If you must, by whom, for whom, you will die.
You are snoring. (The hound of thought by every breath
Brings you nearer for us to your foreign death.)

Are you going? Good-bye, then, to that last word you spoke.
We must try to remember you best by some happy joke.

RETREAT

That is not war—oh it hurts! I am lame.
A thorn is burning me.
We are going back to the place from which we came.
I remember the old song now:

Soldier, soldier, going to war,
When will you come back?

Mind that rut. It is very deep.
All these ways are parched and raw.
Where are we going? How we creep!
Are you there? I never saw—

Damn this jingle in my brain.
I'm full of old songs—Have you ever heard this?

All the roads to victory
Are flooded as we go.
There's so much blood to paddle through,
That's why we're marching slow.

Yes sir; I'm here. Are you an officer?
I can't see. Are we running away?
How long have we done it? One whole year,
A month, a week, or since yesterday?

Damn the jingle. My brain
Is scragged and banged—

Fellows, these are happy times;
Tramp and tramp with open eyes.
Yet, try however much you will,
You cannot see a tree, a hill,
Moon, stars, or even skies.

I won't be quiet. Sing too, you fool.
I had a dog I used to beat.
Don't try it on me. Say that again.
Who said it? *Halt!* Why? Who can halt?
We're marching now. Who fired? Well. Well.
I'll lie down too. I'm tired enough.

IV

CARRION

It is plain now what you are. Your head has dropped
Into a furrow. And the lovely curve
Of your strong leg has wasted and is propped
Against a ridge of the ploughed land's watery swerve.

You are swayed on waves of the silent ground;
You clutch and claim with passionate grasp of your fingers
The dip of earth in which your body lingers;
If you are not found,
In a little while your limbs will fall apart;
The birds will take some, but the earth will take most

your heart.

You are fuel for a coming spring if they leave you here;
The crop that will rise from your bones is healthy bread.
You died—we know you—without a word of fear,
And as they loved you living I love you dead.

No girl would kiss you. But then
No girls would ever kiss the earth
In the manner they hug the lips of men:
You are not known to them in this, your second birth.

No coffin-cover now will cram
Your body in a shell of lead;
Earth will not fall on you from the spade with a slam,
But will fold and enclose you slowly, you living dead.

Hush, I hear the guns. Are you still asleep?
Surely I saw you a little heave to reply.
I can hardly think you will not turn over and creep
Along the furrows trenchward as if to die.

1914

LAMENT IN 1915 (B.H.W.)

I call you, and I call you. Oh come home,
You lonely creature. Curse the foreign clown
Who plugged you with that lead, and knocked you down.
Stand up again and laugh, you wandering friend;
Say, as you would: "It's just a little hole;
It will soon mend."
Walk now into the room. Come! Come! Come! Come!

Come! we will laugh together all the night.
(We shall have poured ourselves a glass or two.)
Sit down. Our mutual mirth will reach its height
When we remember how they called you dead,
And I shall ask you how it felt, and you—
"Oh, nothing. Just a tumble. Rather hot,
The feeling in my side; and then my head
A trifle dizzy, but I'm back again.
I lay out there too long, and I've still got,
When I think of it, just a little pain."

I know the way you tumbled. . . . Once you slid
And landed on your side. I noticed then
A trick of falling; some peculiar glide—
A curious movement, not like other men.
But did your mouth drop open? Did your breath
Hurt you? What sort of feeling quickly came,
When you discovered that it might be death?

And what will happen if I shout your name?
Perhaps you may be there behind the door,
And if I raise my voice a little more,
You'll swing it open. I don't know how thick
The black partition is between us two.
Answer, if you can hear me; friend, be quick. . . .
Listen, the door-bell rang! Perhaps it's you.

You're in the room. You're sitting in that chair.
You are! . . . I will go down. It *was* the bell.
You *may* be waiting at the door as well.

Am I not certain I shall find you there? . . .

You're rigged in your best uniform to-day;
You take a momentary martial stand,
Then step inside and hold me out your hand,
And laugh in that old solitary way.

You don't know why you did it. All this while
You've slaved and sweated. Now you're very strong,
And so you tell me with a knowing smile:
"We're going out to Flanders before long."
I thought you'd come back with an ugly hole
Below your thigh,
And ask for sympathy and wander lame;
I thought you'd be that same
Grumbling companion without self-control—
I never thought you'd die.

.   .   .   .   .

Now let us both forget this brief affair:
Let us begin our friendship all again.
I'm going down to meet you on the stair.
Walk to me! Come! for I can see you plain.
How strange! A moment I did think you dead.
How foolish of me!
Friend! friend! Are you dumb?
Why are you pale? Why do you hang your head?
You see me? Here's my hand. Why don't you come?
Don't make me angry. You are there, I know.
Is not my house your house? There is a bed
Upstairs. You're tired. Lie down; you must come home.
Some men are killed . . . not you. Be as you were.
And yet—Somehow it's dark down all the stair.
I'm standing at the door. You are not there.

1915

TREES

I

One summer afternoon, you find
Some lonely trees. Persuade your mind
To drowse. Then, as your eyelids close,
And you still hover into those
Three stages of a darkening doze,
This side the barrier of sleep,
Pause. In that last clear moment open quick
Your sight toward where the green is bright and thick.
Be sure that everything you keep
To dream with is made out of trees.
Grip hard, become a root, so drive
Your muscles through the ground alive
That you'll be breaking from above your knees
Out into branches. Let your manhood be
Forgotten, your whole purpose seem
The purpose of a simple tree
Rooted in a quiet dream.

I did that. It is difficult to cease
Thinking. A thought will rise and trip
Your spirit on the brink of peace,
So your tough muscles lose their grip.
It will be hard to find
A way to lead you out of Mind,
And after that to keep
The passage of a natural sleep.

(Any silly man can swim
Down the channel of a dream,
Dawdling under banks of green.
That's an easy drift for him,
Snoozing like a little stream,
And a comfortable whim
Any shallow man can dream.
Water is a lazy thing,

Lipping at an edge of ground,
Elbowing and muttering.
I have heard a little stream
Imitate a human dream.)

The trees throw up their singing leaves, and climb
Spray over spray. They break through Time.
Their roots lash through the clay. They lave
The earth, and wash along the ground;
They burst in green wave over wave,
Fly in a blossom of light foam;
Rank following windy rank they come:
They flood the plain,
Swill through the valley, top the mound,
Flow over the low hill,
Curl round
The bases of the mountains, fill
Their crevices, and stain
Their ridges green. . . . Be sure you keep
Some memory of this for sleep.
Then hold your blood, contrive to fill
Your veins with sap. Now dive; now sink
Below the spray. Relax your will. . . .
The earth still has you by the heel?
(Do not remember what you feel!) . . .
Lift up your head above the spray.
Pull (so trees live). Thrust! Drive your way!
The agony of One Idea will twist
Your branches. (Can you feel the dew?)
The wind will cuff you with his fist.
The birds will build their nests in you.
Your circulating blood will go
Flowing five hundred times more slow.
A thousand veils will darkly press
About your muffled consciousness:
So will you grow;
You will not know,
Nor wonder, why you grow. . . .

II

I was cast up from that still tide of sleep,
I suddenly awakened—could not keep
A tranquil growth.
I heard the swinging clocks of man:
And I was conscious of unworthy sloth.
Oh, silly tree-adept!—
Out of arboreal delight I crept;
Crept, was afraid, and ran—
Too much mortality I kept.

They drove me forth. The angry trees
Roared till I tumbled lean and lewd
Out of their Paradise. The forest rose
To scourge my wavering conscience, and pursued.
A thousand doors clapped roughly and were close.
Low growling voices on that other side
Cursed in a tone of old offended wood. . . .

III

It is a dangerous journey. If you go
Think carefully of this, which now I know .—
Tree-growth is but a corridor between
The Seen and the Unseen.
Trees are like sentinels that keep
The passage of a gate
From this sleep to that other sleep:
Between two worlds they wait.
If they discover you, you cannot hide.
Run backward. They are stern.
You may be driven out that other side,
And not return.

Better perhaps you love them distantly—
So if they tempt you, as a woman might,
Make of their love an Immorality;

And if they haunt you, regulate your sight
That tree-love may seem like Adultery;
And never visit them at all by night.
Lock door, draw curtains, close yourself within
When the cool flow of sunset shall begin:
Leave them to float alone about their gold.
But when the moon comes to them and they fold
Dark branches round her, you'll be jealous then—
Focus your vision and contract it near:
Read some new book, talk leisurely with men.
Banish their nightingales, and yet I fear
How they may call and echo through your sleep. . . .
There will be many sounds you must not hear
If you would keep
The ways of manly wisdom, and not be
Distracted by the love of any tree.

There are some men, of course, some men, I know,
Who, when they pass,
Seem like trees walking, and to grow
From earth, and, native in the grass,
(So taut their muscles) move on gliding roots.
They blossom every day: their fruits
Are always new and cover the happy ground.
Wherever they may stand
You hear inevitable sound
Of birds and branches, harvest and all delights
Of pastured and wooded land.
For them it is not dangerous to go
Each side that barrier moving to and fro:
They without trepidation undertake
Excursions into sleep, and safely come awake.

But it is different, different for me,
(Also for you I fear)
To whom a tree seems something more than tree,
And when we see,
Clustered together, two or three,

We almost are afraid to pass them near.
How beautifully they grow,
Above their stiles and lanes and watery places,
Crowding the brink of silence everywhere,
With branches dipping low
To smile toward us or to stroke our faces.
They drown us in their summer, and swirl round,
Leaving us faint: so nobody is free,
But always some surrounding ground
Is swamped and washed and covered in by tree.

They follow us and haunt us. We must build
Houses of wood. Our evening rooms are filled
With fragments of the forest: chairs and tables.
We swing our wooden doors;
Pile up, divide our sheds, byres, stables
With logs, make wooden stairs, lay wooden floors,
Sit, move, and sleep among the limbs of trees,
Rejoicing to be near them. How men saw,
Chisel and hammer, carve and tease
All timber to their purpose, modelling
The forest in their chambers. And the raw
Wild stuff, built like a cupboard or a shelf,
Will crack and shiver in the night, and sing,
Reminding everybody of itself;
Out of decayed old centuries will bring
A sudden memory
Of growing tree.

IV

And they are felled. The hatchet swings:
They pass their way. . . . Some learn to sail
Seaward on white enormous wings,
Scattering blossom along their trail;
Or be a little ship that ploughs
And glides across the rippled land,
Great frothing steeds high mounted at the bows,

Calm at the helm the ploughboy's guiding hand,
Crowded with sailing birds that flap and float,
Hang stiff against the air and hold the breeze,
Landworthy, and as trim a boat
As ever ploughed the seas.

So they are felled. . . . They change, they come,
Lingering their period of decay
In transitory forms; and some
Lie Sleeping all that shining Way
The lanky greyhound engines loop,
With open nostrils flashing by,
Lugging their drowsy noisy troupe—
They clank and clatter, crouch and cry,
Pass, vanish, fill the distance with a sigh.

And some, some trees, before they die,
Carved and moulded small,
Suddenly begin,
Oh, what a wild and windy woodland call
Out of the lips of the violin!

So trees are felled. . . . But Tree
Lingers immovably where it has stood,
Living its tranquil immortality
Impassive to the death of wood.

And you—be certain that you keep
Some memory of trees for sleep.

1915

WEEK-END

I

The train! The twelve o'clock for paradise.
  Hurry, or it will try to creep away.
Out in the country everyone is wise:
  We can be only wise on Saturday.
There you are waiting, little friendly house:
  Those are your chimney-stacks with you between,
Surrounded by old trees and strolling cows,
  Staring through all your windows at the green.
Your homely floor is creaking for our tread;
  The smiling teapot with contented spout
Thinks of the boiling water, and the bread
  Longs for the butter. All their hands are out
      To greet us, and the gentle blankets seem
      Purring and crooning: "Lie in us, and dream."

II

The key will stammer, and the door reply,
  The hall wake, yawn, and smile; the torpid stair
Will grumble at our feet, the table cry:
  "Fetch my belongings for me; I am bare."
A clatter! Something in the attic falls.
  A ghost has lifted up his robes and fled.
The loitering shadows move along the walls;
  Then silence very slowly lifts his head.
The starling with impatient screech has flown
  The chimney, and is watching from the tree.
They thought us gone for ever: mouse alone
  Stops in the middle of the floor to see.
      Now all you idle things, resume your toil.
      Hearth, put your flames on. Sulky kettle, boil.

III

Contented evening; comfortable joys;
   The snoozing fire, and all the fields are still:
Tranquil delight, no purpose, and no noise—
   Unless the slow wind flowing round the hill.
"Murry" (the kettle) dozes; little mouse
   Is rambling prudently about the floor.
There's lovely conversation in this house:
   Words become princes that were slaves before.
What a sweet atmosphere for you and me
   The people that have been here left behind. . . .
Oh, but I fear it may turn out to be
   Built of a dream, erected in the mind:
      So if we speak too loud, we may awaken
      To find it vanished, and ourselves mistaken.

IV

Lift up the curtain carefully. All the trees
   Stand in the dark like drowsy sentinels.
The oak is talkative to-night; he tells
   The little bushes crowding at his knees
That formidable, hard, voluminous
   History of growth from acorn into age.
They titter like school-children; they arouse
   Their comrades, who exclaim: "He is very sage."
Look how the moon is staring through that cloud,
   Laying and lifting idle streaks of light.
O hark! was that the monstrous wind, so loud
   And sudden, prowling always through the night?
      Let down the shaking curtain. They are queer,
      Those foreigners. They and we live so near.

V

Come, come to bed. The shadows move about,
  And someone seems to overhear our talk.
The fire is low; the candles flicker out;
  The ghosts of former tenants want to walk.
Already they are shuffling through the gloom.
  I felt an old man touch my shoulder-blade;
Once he was married here: they love this room,
  He and his woman and the child they made.
Dead, dead, they are, yet some familiar sound,
  Creeping along the brink of happy life,
Revives their memory from under ground—
  The farmer and his troublesome old wife.
        Let us be going: as we climb the stairs,
        They'll sit down in our warm half-empty chairs.

VI

Morning! Wake up! Awaken! All the boughs
  Are rippling on the air across the green.
The youngest birds are singing to the house.
  Blood of the world!—and is the country clean?
Disturb the precinct. Cool it with a shout.
  Sing as you trundle down to light the fire.
Turn the encumbering shadows tumbling out,
  And fill the chambers with a new desire.
Life is no good, unless the morning brings
  White happiness and quick delight of day.
These half-inanimate domestic things
  Must all be useful, or must go away.
        Coffee, be fragrant. Porridge in my plate,
        Increase the vigour to fulfil my fate.

VII

The fresh air moves like water round a boat.
　　The white clouds wander. Let us wander too.
The whining wavering plover flap and float.
　　That crow is flying after that cuckoo.
Look! Look! . . . They're gone. What are the
　　　　　　　　　　　　great trees calling?
　　Just come a little farther, by that edge
Of green, to where the stormy ploughland, falling
　　Wave upon wave, is lapping to the hedge.
Oh, what a lovely bank! Give me your hand.
　　Lie down and press your heart against the ground.
Let us both listen till we understand,
　　Each through the other, every natural sound. . . .

　　　　　I can't hear anything to-day, can you,
　　　　　But, far and near: "Cuckoo! Cuckoo! Cuckoo!"?

VIII

The everlasting grass—how bright, how cool!
　　The day has gone too suddenly, too soon.
There's something white and shiny in that pool—
　　Throw in a stone, and you will hit the moon.
Listen, the church-bell ringing! Do not say
　　We must go back to-morrow to our work.
We'll tell them we are dead: we died to-day.
　　We're lazy. We're too happy. We will shirk.
We're cows. We're kettles. We'll be anything
　　Except the manikins of time and fear.
We'll start away to-morrow wandering,
　　And nobody will notice in a year. . . .
　　　　　Now the great sun is slipping under ground.
　　　　　Grip firmly!—How the earth is whirling round.

IX

Be staid; be careful; and be not too free.
　　Temptation to enjoy your liberty
May rise against you, break into a crime,
　　And smash the habit of employing Time.
It serves no purpose that the careful clock
　　Mark the appointment, the officious train
Hurry to keep it, if the minutes mock
　　Loud in your ear: "Late. Late. Late. Late again."
Week-end is very well on Saturday:
　　On Monday it's a different affair—
A little episode, a trivial stay
　　In some oblivious spot somehow, somewhere.
　　　　On Sunday night we hardly laugh or speak:
　　　　Week-end begins to merge itself in Week.

X

Pack up the house, and close the creaking door.
　　The fields are dull this morning in the rain.
It's difficult to leave that homely floor.
　　Wave a light hand; we will return again.
(What was that bird?) Good-bye, ecstatic tree,
　　Floating, bursting, and breathing on the air.
The lonely farm is wondering that we
　　Can leave. How every window seems to stare!
That bag is heavy. Share it for a bit.
　　You like that gentle swashing of the ground
As we tread? . . .
　　　　　　It is over. Now we sit
Reading the morning paper in the sound
　　　　Of the debilitating heavy train.
　　　　London again, again. London again.

1915–16

64

STRANGE MEETINGS

I

If suddenly a clod of earth should rise,
And walk about, and breathe, and speak, and love,
How one would tremble, and in what surprise
    Gasp: "Can *you* move?"

I see men walking, and I always feel:
"Earth! How have you done this? What can you be?"
I can't learn how to know men, or conceal
How strange they are to me.

II

The dark space underneath is full of bones,
The surface filled with bodies—roving men,
And floating above the surface a foam of eyes:
Over that is Heaven. All the Gods
Walk with cool feet, paddle among the eyes;
Scatter them like foam-flakes on the wind
Over the human world.

III

Rising toward the surface, we are men
A moment, till we dive again, and then
We take our ease of breathing: we are sent
Unconscious to our former element,
There being perfect, living without pain
Till we emerge like men, and meet again.

IV

You live there; I live here:
Other people everywhere
Haunt their houses, and endure

Days and deeds and furniture,
Circumstances, families,
And the stare of foreign eyes.

V

Often we must entertain,
Tolerantly if we can,
Ancestors returned again
Trying to be modern man.
Gates of Memory are wide;
All of them can shuffle in,
Join the family, and, once inside,
Alas, what a disturbance they begin!
Creatures of another time and mood,
They wrangle; they dictate;
Bawl their experience into brain and blood,
Call themselves *Fate*.

VI

Eyes float above the surface, trailing
Obedient bodies, lagging feet.
Where the wind of words is wailing
Eyes and voices part and meet.

VII

BIRTH
One night when I was in the House of Death,
A shrill voice penetrated root and stone,
And the whole earth was shaken under ground:
I woke and there was light above my head.

Before I heard that shriek I had not known
The region of Above from Underneath,
Alternate light and dark, silence and sound,
Difference between the living and the dead.

It is difficult to tell
(Though we feel it well),
How the surface of the land
Budded into head and hand:
But it is a great surprise
How it blossomed into eyes.

IX

A flower is looking through the ground,
Blinking at the April weather;
Now a child has seen the flower:
Now they go and play together.

Now it seems the flower will speak,
And will call the child its brother—
But, oh strange forgetfulness!—
They don't recognise each other.

X

Yesterday I heard a thrush;
He held me with his eyes:
I waited on my yard of earth,
He watched me from his skies.

My whole day was penetrated
By his wild and windy cries,
And the glitter of his eyes.

XI

The stars must make an awful noise
In whirling round the sky;

Yet somehow I can't even hear
Their loudest song or sigh.

So it is wonderful to think
One blackbird can outsing
The voice of all the swarming stars
On any day in spring.

XII

Oh, how reluctantly some people learn
To hold their bones together, with what toil
Breathe and are moved, as though they would return,
How gladly, and be crumbled into soil!

They knock their groping bodies on the stones,
Blink at the light, and startle at all sound,
With their white lips learn only a few moans,
Then go back under ground.

XIII

The ploughboy, he could never understand—
While he was carried dozing in the cart,
Or strolling with the plough across the land,
He never knew he had a separate heart.

Had someone told him, had he understood,
It would have been like tearing up the ground.
He slowly moves and slowly grows like wood,
And does not turn his head for any sound.

So they mistook him for a clod of land,
And round him, while he dreamed, they built a town.
He rubs his eyes; he cannot understand,
But like a captive wanders up and down.

XIV

You may not ever go to heaven;
You had better love the earth:
You'll achieve, for all your pain,
(What you cannot understand)
Privilege to drive a flower
Through an inch of land.
All the world is in your brain:
Worship it, in human power,
With your body and your hand.

XV

I often stood at my open gate,
　　Watching the passing crowd with no surprise:
I don't think I had used my eyes for hate
　　Till they met your eyes.

I don't believe this road is meant for you,
　　Or, if it be,
Will no one say what I am meant to do
　　Now while you stare at me?

XVI

How did you enter that body? Why are you here?
At once, when I had seen your eyes appear
Over the brim of earth, they were looking for me.
How suddenly, how silently
We rose into this long-appointed place.
From what sleep have you arrived,
That your beauty has survived?
You, the everlasting—you
Known before a word was. . . .

XVII

To-day, when you were sitting in the house,
And I was walking to you from the town,
At the far corner of the alder-wood,
I'm certain you were strolling up and down.

I thought: "She's come to meet me, and meanwhile
Is talking to the cowslips in the dew."
Just as you saw me, and began to smile—
It was not you.

Now I'm not certain—for how shall I say?
I cannot tell, however I may stare,
If it be you here in the house all day,
Or whether you are wandering still out there.

XVIII

Wipe away, please,
That film from your eyes.
I can't see you plainly. Are you
The friend that I seem to remember? Are we
The people I think we must be?
We have talked for an hour: it seems you are he.
I know you, I'm sure, though your eyes are so altered.
Oh, in what life of our lives did we meet?—
But you smile, then you sigh, then you frown:
Now you stare at me angrily. How can it be?
I know you—you do not know me.

XIX

A man who has clung to a branch and he hangs—
    Wondering when it will break.

A woman who sits by the bed of a child,
    Watching for him to wake.

People who gaze at the town-hall clock,
    Waiting to hear the hour.

Somebody walking along a path,
    Stooping to pick a flower.

Dawn; and the reaper comes out of his home,
    Moving along to mow.

A frightened crowd in a little room,
    Waiting all day to go.

A tall man rubbing his eyes in the dusk,
    Muttering "Yes"; murmuring "No."

XX

It is not difficult to die:
You hold your breath and go to sleep;
Your skin turns white or grey or blue,
And some of your relations weep.

The cheerful clock without a pause
Will finish your suspended day.
That body you were building up
Will suddenly be thrown away.

You turn your fingers to the ground,
Drop all the things you had to do:
It is the first time in your life
You'll cease completely to be you.

XXI

Memory opens; memory closes:
Memory taught me to be a man.

It remembers everything:
It helps the little birds to sing.

It finds the honey for the bee:
It opens and closes, opens and closes. . . .

> —*Proverbs for the humble wise;*
> *Flashes out of human eyes;*
> *Oracles of paradise.*

1915–16

CORONILLA

I

Coronilla! Coronilla!
  Heavy yellow tepid bloom:
(Midnight in a scented room)—
  Coronilla.

Southern road; muffled house . . .
  Later on to-night
I'll come again so quietly
  By moonlight.

.   .   .   .   .

Oh, what is that I think I see
  So pale beyond the yellow dusk,
Beyond the trailing bitter flower
  And reek of marrow-bone and musk?

Is it a face?—My frozen hands
  Are hiding in their bone:
The stare above the little mouth;
  And she and I alone.

She calls me. Oh, I wonder why.
  She wants me. Shall I go?
Now is your time, my brain, to cry
  The often-practised *No*.

.   .   .   .   .

Coronilla, I have passed you,
  Seven times a day.
Why do I always take my walk
  The southern way?

Although I hate your bitter reek,
   I still return, and still
Long that your hidden voice may speak
   Against my wavering will.

Wait for me. I will come to-morrow.
   Must you have your way?
Wait, then; I will come to-morrow.
   I am going home to-day.

.   .   .   .   .

Coronilla! Coronilla!
   Are you here to-night?
Seven times I've come to you
   By moonlight.

Now I must feel your tepid bloom.
   I'll twist your tendrils through my skin;
So, if you have a shuttered room,
   Coronilla, let me in.

II

He cooled the hollow of his cheek,
   And filled it with the drowsy flower.
He has become so gentle, weak,
   And feverish in her power.

Now all the sappy little leaves
   Are clinging to his frozen lips;
And she has drawn the shutter back,
   And drawn him with her finger-tips.

The candles flicker in the room.
   He trembles by the wall.
She gave him all and all again,
   But still he asks for all.

So one by one the candles droop
   And close their eyes and faint away.
The yellow blooms begin to stoop:
   He has not noticed it is day.

III

Now he has laid his body down,
   And all his skin is silver pale;
He'll never, never rise again:
   His muscles have begun to fail.

He's covered with a winding sheet.
   There's yet a little time to rave,
Then he will hear the grains of earth
   Drip-dropping on his grave.

Yellow, yellow is the flower;
   Fatal is the bloom;
And no one any time returned
   Who slept inside the shuttered room.

1913–16

SOLITUDE

When you have tidied all things for the night,
And while your thoughts are fading to their sleep,
You'll pause a moment in the late firelight,
Too sorrowful to weep.

The large and gentle furniture has stood
In sympathetic silence all the day,
With that old kindness of domestic wood;
Nevertheless the haunted room will say:
"Someone must be away."

The little dog rolls over half awake,
Stretches his paws, yawns, looking up at you,
Wags his tail very slightly for your sake,
That you may feel he is unhappy too.

A distant engine whistles, or the floor
Creaks, or the wandering night-wind bangs a door.

Silence is scattered like a broken glass.
The minutes prick their ears and run about,
Then one by one subside again and pass
Sedately in, monotonously out.

You bend your head and wipe away a tear.
Solitude walks one heavy step more near.

1916

ASPIDISTRA STREET

Go along that road, and look at sorrow.
Every window grumbles.
All day long the drizzle fills the puddles,
Trickles in the runnels and the gutters,
Drips and drops and dripples, drops and dribbles,
While the melancholy aspidistra
Frowns between the parlour curtains.

Uniformity, dull Master!—
Birth and marriage, middle-age and death;
Rain and gossip: Sunday, Monday, Tuesday . . .

Sure, the lovely fools who made Utopia
Planned it without any aspidistra.
There will be a heaven on earth, but first
We must banish from the parlour
Plush and poker-work and paper flowers,
Brackets, staring photographs and what-nots,
Serviettes, frills and etageres,
Anti-macassars, vases, chiffoniers;

And the gloomy aspidistra
Glowering through the window-pane,
Meditating heavy maxims,
Moralising to the rain.

1916

OFFICERS' MESS (1916)

I

I search the room with all my mind
Peering among those eyes;
For I am feverish to find
A brain with which my brain may talk,
Not that I think myself too wise,
But that I'm lonely, and I walk
Round the large place and wonder—No:
There's nobody, I fear,
Lonely as I, and here.

How they hate me. I'm a fool.
I can't play Bridge; I'm bad at Pool;
I cannot drone a comic song;
I can't talk Shop; I can't use Slang;
My jokes are bad, my stories long:
My voice will falter, break or hang,
Not blurt the sour sarcastic word,
And so my swearing sounds absurd.

II

But came the talk: I found
Three or four others for an argument.
I forced their pace. They shifted their dull ground,
And went
Sprawling about the passages of Thought.
We tugged each other's words until they tore.
They asked me my philosophy: I brought
Bits of it forth and laid them on the floor.
They laughed, and so I kicked the bits about,
Then put them in my pocket one by one,
I, sorry I had brought them out,
They, grateful for the fun.

And when these words had thus been sent
Jerking about, like beetles round a wall,
Then one by one to dismal sleep we went:
There was no happiness at all
In that short hopeless argument
Through yawns and on the way to bed
Among men waiting to be dead.

1916

REAL PROPERTY

Tell me about that harvest field.
Oh! Fifty acres of living bread.
The colour has painted itself in my heart.
The form is patterned in my head.

So now I take it everywhere;
See it whenever I look round;
Hear it growing through every sound,
Know exactly the sound it makes—
Remembering, as one must all day,
Under the pavement the live earth aches.

Trees are at the farther end,
Limes all full of the mumbling bee:
So there must be a harvest field
Whenever one thinks of a linden tree.

A hedge is about it, very tall,
Hazy and cool, and breathing sweet.
Round paradise is such a wall
And all the day, in such a way,
In paradise the wild birds call.

You only need to close your eyes
And go within your secret mind,
And you'll be into paradise:
I've learnt quite easily to find
Some linden trees and drowsy bees,
A tall sweet hedge with the corn behind.

I will not have that harvest mown:
I'll keep the corn and leave the bread.
I've bought that field; it's now my own:
I've fifty acres in my head.
I take it as a dream to bed.
I carry it about all day. . . .

Sometimes when I have found a friend
I give a blade of corn away.

1916

FATE

I

I have so often
Examined all this well-known room
That I inhabit.

There is the open window;
There the locked door, the door I cannot open,
The only doorway.

When at the keyhole often, often
I bend and listen, I can always hear
A muffled conversation.

An argument:
An angry endless argument of people
Who live behind;

Some loudly talking,
Some dimly into separate conflict moving,
Behind the door.

There they seem prisoned,
As I, in this lone room that I inhabit:
My life; my body.

You, of the previous Being,
You who once made me, and who now discuss me,
Tell me your edict.

You, long ago,
With doubting hands and eager trembling fingers,
Prepared my room.

Before I came,
Each gave a token for remembrance, left it,
And then retired behind the bolted door.

There is the pot of honey
One brought, and there the jar of vinegar
On the same table.

Who poured that water
Shining beside the flask of yellow wine?
Who sighed so softly?

Who brought that living flower to the room?
Who groaned—and I can ever hear the echo?
—You do not answer.

Meanwhile from out the distance
Sounds reach me as of building other houses:
Men building houses.

And if they ever
Should open up a doorway in the wall,
And I pass onward,

What should I take them
Beyond those doorways, in the other rooms?
What shall I bring them,
That they may love me?

Fatal question!
For all the jangling voices rise together:
"What should he take them?"

"What shall he take them?"
Through that locked door there is no final answer.
They are debating, endlessly debating . . . .

II

O Fate! Have you no other gift
Than voices in a muffled room?
Why do you live behind a door,
And hide yourself in gloom?

And why, again, should you not have
One purpose only, one sole word,
Ringing for ever round my heart:
Plainly delivered, plainly heard?

Your conversation fills my brain
And tortures all my life, and yet
Gives nothing, and I often think
You've grown so old, that you forget;

And having learnt man's fatal trick
Of talking, talking, talking still,
You're tired of definite design,
And laugh at having lost your Will.

1920

THE GARDEN

He told me he had seen a ruined garden
Outside the town.
"Where? Where?"
I asked him quickly.
He said it lay toward the southern country;
He knew the road well: he would take me there.

Then he sat down and talked
About that garden.
He was so grandly proud and sure of it,
I listened all the evening to his talk.

And our glasses were emptied,
Talking of it.
We filled them and filled them again,
Talking of it.

He said that no one knew
The garden but himself;
Though hundreds passed it day by day,
Yet no one knew it but himself.

I

The garden, it was long and wide
And filled with great unconscious peace;
All the old trees were tall and large,
And all the birds—

The birds, he said, were like a choir
Of lively boys,
Who never went to school,
But sang instead.

He told me of the trailing flowers
Hung on the ruined walls;

The rivers and their waterfalls;
The hidden woods; the lawns; the bowers.

Small cool plantations; palm and vine,
With fig-tree growing by their side,
And violet and maidenhair
And

II

we were late in conversation
Talking of that most wonderful garden,
And filled our glasses again and again
Talking about that beautiful garden,

Until he vowed in the middle of drink
To lead me to-morrow to see it myself.
We closed our hands on the pact.
He vanished away through the dark.

III

To-morrow, to-morrow, we start our walk.
To-morrow is here and he meets me surely.
Out from the city we go and pursue
Mile after mile of the open road;

Come to a place of sudden trees,
Pass it across the fields, then on
By farmyards, through villages, over the downs:

Mile after mile we walk. He is pleased.
Our feet become heavy with dust, and we laugh,
And we talk all the while of our future delight.

IV

He came upon the garden in the dusk;

He leaned against the wall:
He pointed out its beauties in the gloom.
We lay down weary in the shadow of elms,
And stared between their branches at the moon,
And talked about to-morrow and the garden.
I knew that everything he said was true,
For we were resting up against the wall.

V

Oh hard awakening from a dream:
I thought I was in paradise.
He cooked the coffee we had brought,
Then looked about him.

We had not reached the wall, he found.
It was a little farther on.
We walked another mile or two,
And stood before the ruined gate.

He was not satisfied at all.
He said the entrance was not here.
I hardly understood his talk,
And so I watched him move about.
Indeed, it was the garden he had meant;
But not the one he had described.

VI

Then suddenly from out his conversation
I saw it in the light of his own thought:
A phantom Eden shining
Placid among his dreams.

And he, with large eyes and with hands uplifted,
Cried: "Look, O look!" Indeed I saw the garden;
The ghostly palm and violet,
Fig, maidenhair, and fountain;

The rivers and their flowered lawns; the gleaming
Birds; and their song—I heard that clear I know.
And silent, in amazement,
We stared

Then both sat down beneath the wall and rested,
And in our conversation
Lived in the garden.

VII

"We'll come again next week," he said at last.
"We have no leisure to explore it now;
Besides we cannot climb this crumbling wall:
Our gate is on the farther side, I know.
We'd have to go right round, and even then
I am not sure it's open till the spring.
I have affairs in town. If you don't mind,
We will go back directly. After all,
The garden cannot run away, or change.
Next week I'll have more time, and, once inside,
Who knows . . . who knows? How very curious too,
Hundreds of people pass it day by day
Along that high road over there; the cars—
Look at them! And the railway too! Well. Well,
I'm glad that no one cares for Eden now.
It would be spoilt so quickly. We'll go back
By train, if you don't mind. I've walked enough.
Look, there's the station. Eh?"

VIII

I did not see that man again
Until a year had gone or more.
I had not found him anywhere,
And many times had gone to seek
The garden, but it was not there.

One day along the country road
There was he coming all alone.
He would have passed me with a stare.
I held his arm, but he was cold,
And rudely asked me my affair.
I said, there was a garden, I'd been told . . .

IX

Then suddenly came that rapture upon us;
We saw the garden again in our mutual thought:
Blue and yellow and green,
Shining by day or by night.

"Those are the trees," he said, "and there is the gateway.
To-day, I think, it is open. And shall we not go there?"
Quickly we ran in our joy;
Quickly—then stopped, and stared.

X

An angel with a flaming sword
Stood large, and beautiful, and clear:
He covered up his golden eyes,
And would not look as we came near.

Birds wheeled about the flowery gate,
But we could never see inside,
Although (I often think) it stood
Slack on its hinges open wide.

The angel dropped his hopeless sword,
And stood with his great pinions furled,
And wept into his hands: but we
Feared, and turned back to our own world.

1920

INTROSPECTION

That house across the road is full of ghosts;
The windows, all inquisitive, look inward:
All are shut.
I've never seen a body in the house;
Have you? Have you?
Yet feet go sounding in the corridors,
And up and down, and up and down the stairs,
All day, all night, all day.

When will the show begin?
When will the host be in?
What is the preparation for?
When will he open the bolted door?
When will the minutes move smoothly along
                          in their hours?
Time, answer!

The air must be hot: how hot inside.
If only somebody could go
And snap the windows open wide,
And keep them so!

All the back rooms are very large, and there
(So it is said)
They sit before their open books and stare;
Or one will rise and sadly shake his head;
Another will but comb and comb her hair,
While some will move untiringly about
Through all the rooms, for ever in and out,
Or up and down the stair;

Or gaze into the small back-garden
And talk about the rain,
Then drift back from the window to the table,
Folding long hands, to sit and think again.

They do never meet like homely people
Round a fireside
After daily work . . .
Always busy with procrastination,
Backward and forward they move in the house,
Full of questions
No one can answer.
Nothing will happen. . . . Nothing will happen. . . .

c 1920

THE SILENT POOL

I

I have discovered finally to-day
This house that I have called my own
Is built of straw and clay,
Not, as I thought, of stone.

I wonder who the architect could be,
What builder made it of that stuff;
When it was left to me
The house seemed good enough.

Yet, slowly, as its roof began to sink,
And as its walls began to split,
And I began to think,
Then I suspected it;

But did not clearly know until to-day
That it was only built of straw and clay.

II

Now I will go about on my affairs
As though I had no cares,
Nor ever think at all
How one day soon that house is bound to fall,
So when I'm told the wind has blown it down
I may have something else to call my own.

I have enquired who was the architect,
What builder did erect.
I'm told they did design
Million and million others all like mine,
And argument with all men ends the same:—
It is impossible to fix the blame.

I am so glad that underneath our talk
Our minds together walk.
We argue all the while,
But down below our argument we smile.
We have our houses, but we understand
That our real property is common land.

III

At night we often go
With happy comrades to that real estate,
Where dreams in beauty grow,
And every man enjoys a common fate.

At night in sleep one flows
Below the surface of all argument;
The brain, with all it knows,
Is covered by the waters of content.

But when the dawn appears
Brain rises to the surface with a start,
And, waking, quickly sneers
At the old natural brightness of the heart.

Oh, that a man might choose
To live unconsciously like beast or bird,
And our clear thought not lose
Its beauty when we turn it into word.

IV

Those quarrellings between my brain and heart
(In which I'd take no part)
Pursue their violent course
Corrupting my most vital force
So that my natural property is spent
In fees to keep alive their argument.

V

Look downward in the silent pool:
The weeds cling to the ground they love;
They live so quietly, are so cool;
They do not need to think, or move.

Look down in the unconscious mind:
There everything is quiet too
And deep and cool, and you will find
Calm growth and nothing hard to do,
And nothing that need trouble you.

c 1921

THE EARTH FOR SALE

I

How perilous life will become on earth
When the great breed of man has covered all.
The world, that was too large, will be too small.
Deserts and mountains will have been explored,
Valleys swarmed through; and our prolific breed,
Exceeding death ten million times by birth,
Will halt (bewildered, bored),
And then may droop and dwindle like an autumn weed.

How shall we meet that moment when we know
There is no room to grow;
We, conscious, and with lonely startled eyes
Glaring upon ourselves, and with no Lord
To pray to: judged, without appeal,
What shall we feel?
He, being withdrawn, no supplicating cries
Will call Him back. He'll speak no farther word.

Can special vision be required to see
What few pale centuries will take us there,
Where, at the barrier of the future, we
Shall stand condemned, in serried ranks, and stare
At Nothing—fearing Something may appear?

The Earth is covered with large auction boards,
And all her lands are reckoned up for sale.
The spaces that are now called virgin soil
Will soon be bought, and covered with great breed
Of human seed;
And, when the driven hordes
Cry "Food!"—but find no more for any toil,
Fear, fear will strike all eyes and faces pale.

MAN CARRYING BALE

The tough hand closes gently on the load;
  Out of the mind, a voice
Calls "Lift!" and the arms, remembering well their work,
  Lengthen and pause for help.
Then a slow ripple flows along the body,
While all the muscles call to one another:
  "Lift!" and the bulging bale
  Floats like a butterfly in June.

So moved the earliest carrier of bales,
  And the same watchful sun
Glowed through his body feeding it with light.
  So will the last one move,
And halt, and dip his head, and lay his load
Down, and the muscles will relax and tremble. . . .
  Earth, you designed your man
  Beautiful both in labour, and repose.

UNKNOWN COUNTRY

Here, in this other world, they come and go
With easy dream-like movements to and fro.
They stare through lovely eyes, yet do not seek
An answering gaze, or that a man should speak.
Had I a load of gold, and should I come
Bribing their friendship, and to buy a home,
They would stare harder and would slightly frown:
I am a stranger from the distant town.

Oh, with what patience I have tried to win
The favour of the hostess of the Inn!
Have I not offered toast on frothing toast
Looking toward the melancholy host;
Praised the old wall-eyed mare to please the groom;
Laughed to the laughing maid and fetched her broom;
Stood in the background not to interfere
When the cool ancients frolicked at their beer;
Talked only in my turn, and made no claim
For recognition or by voice or name,
Content to listen, and to watch the blue
Or grey of eyes, or what good hands can do?

Sun-freckled lads, who at the dusk of day
Stroll through the village with a scent of hay
Clinging about you from the windy hill,
Why do you keep your secret from me still?
You loiter at the corner of the street:
I in the distance silently entreat.
I know too well I'm city-soiled, but then
So are to-day ten million other men.
My heart is true: I've neither will nor charms
To lure away your maidens from your arms.
Trust me a little. Must I always stand
Lonely, a stranger from an unknown land?

There is a riddle here. Though I'm more wise
Than you, I cannot read your simple eyes.
I find the meaning of their gentle look
More difficult than any learned book.
I pass: perhaps a moment you may chaff
My walk, and so dismiss me with a laugh.
I come: you all, most grave and most polite,
Stand silent first, then wish me calm Good-Night.
When I go back to town some one will say:
"I think that stranger must have gone away."
And "Surely!" some one else will then reply.
Meanwhile, within the dark of London, I
Shall, with my forehead resting on my hand,
Not cease remembering your distant land;
Endeavouring to reconstruct aright
How some treed hill has looked in evening light;
Or be imagining the blue of skies
Now as in heaven, now as in your eyes;
Or in my mind confusing looks or words
Of yours with dawnlight, or the song of birds:
Not able to resist, not even keep
Myself from hovering near you in my sleep:
You still as callous to my thought and me
As flowers to the purpose of the bee.

1913-20

Then no one more will speak,
But, rising from a murmur to a wail,
One voice, for all, will, like a Siren, shriek.

II

Is there no pledge to make at once with Earth
While yet we have not murdered all her trees;
Before it is too late for oath or pledge;
While yet man may be happy in his birth—
Before we have to fall upon our knees,
Clinging for safety to her farthest edge?

It is not very noble that we kill
Her lions and tigers, all. Is that our reign?—
Then let us build ourselves on earth again.
What is the human will?

Is it so clearly better than the ant's?
And is our life more holy than the plants'?
They do fulfil their purpose every year,
And bring no pain, nor fear.

III

Woe to that miserable last mankind;
And, when I think of that, I have a dread
I may awake on earth, again, to find
Myself, among it, living, oh, not dead.

IV

I had been thinking of that final Earth.
Then I remembered she herself would lick
Her own lithe body clean, and from her girth
Wipe any vermin that might cling too thick.

Damned! Damned! Apparent conqueror to-day—
Oh, evanescent sway!
O drunken lust!
O swarming dust!

Man makes himself believe he has a claim
To plant bright flags on every hill he swarms;
But in the end, and in his own wild name,
And for the better prospect of his fame,
Whether it be a person or a race,
Earth, with a smiling face,
Will hold and smother him in her large arms.

1922–4

HOLY MATRIMONY

I

It was a fatal trick to play upon him.
With lusty life all pointing to one aim,
And his whole body watchful:
She at the moment came.

Could he resist? Could she? That one blue glance
Was not her own: oh, a far stronger power
Than hers shone at him through her
And fixed their mating hour.

II

Words, hardly needed, then were spoken,
All having only one intent.
They walked like children staring downward,
With body toward body bent.

Now all the others mumble darkly,
Wonder and enviously stare.
There is a glowing in the household:
Desire will dwell a moment here.

But older eyes gleam coldly on them;
Stiffer bodies step between.
Now while the preparations start
They must be cleanly kept apart:
So has the custom always been.

"You cannot kneel before the altar
Until we've trimmed the lamp for you.
Meanwhile you may a little woo;
We've much to do:
We'll bake and sew and watch you sidelong,
And make your wedding bed for you."

III

But he and she
They hear, they stare,
And they are asking:
Who are we?

They cling and cry:
What have we done?
Through us what ceremonial
Is begun?

The dark doors close
Upon the sky.
They shall be locked within
Till they do die.

IV

O prison church! O warder-priest!
Now they who used to walk the wind of freedom
Are living in your gloomy house of stone;
And they and it are growing older;
She is becoming every day less fair.
The more together, they are more alone:
They pile the fire and yet the hearth is colder.

1924

LIVING

Slow bleak awakening from the morning dream
Brings me in contact with the sudden day.
I am alive—this I.
I let my fingers move along my body.
Realisation warns them, and my nerves
Prepare their rapid messages and signals.
While Memory begins recording, coding,
Repeating; all the time Imagination
Mutters: You'll only die.

Here's a new day. O Pendulum move slowly!
My usual clothes are waiting on their peg.
I am alive—this I.
And in a moment Habit, like a crane,
Will bow its neck and dip its pulleyed cable,
Gathering me, my body, and our garment,
And swing me forth, oblivious of my question,
Into the daylight—why?

I think of all the others who awaken,
And wonder if they go to meet the morning
More valiantly than I;
Nor asking of this Day they will be living:
What have I done that I should be alive?
O, can I not forget that I am living?
How shall I reconcile the two conditions:
Living, and yet—to die?

Between the curtains the autumnal sunlight
With lean and yellow finger points me out;
The clock moans: Why? Why? Why?
But suddenly, as if without a reason,
Heart, Brain and Body, and Imagination
All gather in tumultuous joy together,

Running like children down the path of morning
To fields where they can play without a quarrel:
A country I'd forgotten, but remember,
And welcome with a cry.

O cool glad pasture; living tree, tall corn,
Great cliff, or languid sloping sand, cold sea,
Waves; rivers curving: you, eternal flowers,
Give me content, while I can think of you:
Give me your living breath!
Back to your rampart, Death.

1924

MIDNIGHT LAMENTATION

When you and I go down
Breathless and cold,
Our faces both worn back
To earthly mould,
How lonely we shall be!
What shall we do,
You without me,
I without you?

I cannot bear the thought
You, first, may die,
Nor of how you will weep,
Should I.
We are too much alone;
What can we do
To make our bodies one:
You, me; I, you?

We are most nearly born
Of one same kind;
We have the same delight,
The same true mind.
Must we then part, we part;
Is there no way
To keep a beating heart,
And light of day?

I could now rise and run
Through street on street
To where you are breathing—you,
That we might meet,
And that your living voice
Might sound above
Fear, and we two rejoice
Within our love.

How frail the body is,
And we are made
As only in decay
To lean and fade.
I think too much of death;
There is a gloom
When I can't hear your breath
Calm in some room.

O, but how suddenly
Either may droop;
Countenance be so white,
Body stoop.
Then there may be a place
Where fading flowers
Drop on a lifeless face
Through weeping hours.

Is then nothing safe?
Can we not find
Some everlasting life
In our one mind?
I feel it like disgrace
Only to understand
Your spirit through your word,
Or by your hand.

I cannot find a way
Through love and through;
I cannot reach beyond
Body, to you.
When you or I must go
Down evermore,
There'll be no more to say
—But a locked door.

c 1924

DREAM EXHIBITION OF A FINAL WORLD

I

The murky curtains roll apart. A gigantic Proscenium.
  Dawn.
The purple lips of the Siren begin to twitch.
Eastward, a giant arc-light reflects through my dream
Glaringly, into a forest of chimneys.
Heavy upon my chest the large gorilla squats,
Holding, loosely, my throat.

The pulley-sinewed God of Earth whose arm is like a crane
Now will lever the cable to open the lip of the Siren.
She mutters; her great head is wobbling:
Then her cry
Rattles her throat, before rising through pouted mouth
To a whistle, a warble, a wild full blast and a shriek;
Now a screech as her cheeks puff out; and it gashes the light.
Her hair in the wind of her howl is frayed on the sky.

Early dreaming-time has guttered away.
She dwindles. Her lips, her eyes are closing.
The light of morning hangs in ribbons, bulging.
Now the charabancs marshalled in regiments with hooter
    roaring
Thunder around the earth, round the Great Exhibition.
Aeroplanes flood the sky writing the news, and heaven
Films to the world, and winks. Within the electric proscenium
There shall be dawn every day, imitated;
Whatever the season, beautiful, artificial,
Such as the Worker loves, bright like a picture postcard.

The exhibition was planned to endure through final humanity.
(Hefty gorilla, lift your claws from my throat,
  Lurking ancestor phantom of final world,
  Pranked in a purple Top-hat.)

II

The Gate is rare and precious,
Built of granite, the last to be quarried on earth,
Guarded by armies of negroes pranked in helmets of scarlet.
Not far within are kept, in golden cages,
Small broods, diminishing, of those old beasts:
Last lion of earth, last tiger, rhinoceros, buffalo;
In marble tank the last large whale of ocean.
Honoured: each has a lecturer talking
Glibly of habit and haunt, day and night, day and night.
Here is a tiny forest, reared by an old-world expert,
Fanned, that it whisper well, by regulated zephyrs;
Near to which in a cage on wheels, lined with satin and moss,
To be moved at his mood, and filled with mechanical birds,
There lives, walking up and down, in tweed, with a stick of
        rarest ash-plant,
Murmuring, making a note, or sipping beer from a tankard,
(Gloated upon by the crowd),
Rarer than lion, or granite, the last, last, Nature Poet.

Beyond is the last great valley (Charabanc, Charabanc, roaring!)
Here are the old cascades,
Warranted still in their ancient courses,
Guaranteed to be haunted yet by the spirit of beauty,
Mumbling mysteriously far within their barb-wire encircled
        enclosures;
And every train-and-villa-girdled mountain
Is crowned with proud hotels.

There stands the last cathedral. Out beyond,
The free and vast asylum of beliefs
(Encooped are they in one gigantic cold enclosure)
Folds all the faithful. They may build therein
Church, Meeting House, Synagogue, Mosque, or Chapel.
Dreamy cranes are waiting without to lift within that arid space,
Complete, ready for use, direct from the factory,
Chapel, church, or cathedral, of corrugated iron.

Under the pulpit where preaches the Pope Himself
Latest American upstart may roar; here Salvation Army
Mass bands. Here rules, at length, the Spirit of Freedom.
For nobody fights any more about any religion.
Nobody troubles the clock-work heart of the God,
Lest cog, chain, piston, crank of the great machine
Should waver to hear or argue, or break, like a heart.

III

But, oh! the Mob is roaring! Here is mob roaring!
Armies (here it is different), armies, howling revenge.
The narrow, enormous arena where rules the downturned
    thumb.
Charabanc massed. Epsom. Telescope, Nero! Nero!
Tank! Bomb! Tank! Bomb! Every Terminus ending here!
Beautiful hail of blood. Millions killed in a minute.
War final, War! Never a shortage of bodies.
Watch the game, heroes! Hurrying clouds of corpses!
(Only a Magnate need gnash his teeth at Another.)
"Card of the War, sir? No seats left.
One in the upper circle. Only a thousand guineas."
Here is the final Circus, here is the final . . .

IV

Gorilla clutching my heart!
Shall I waken at all from the last Exhibition?
Will there be forest again, and sunrise and cornfield, this
    morning,
Farmhouse, haystack, flowers in the garden,
Protective, patient tree, that leans over the roof,
Near the trembling dimpering sea, where the long sand is hot,
And the slow tide rises and falls.
Breezes play lightly through meadows in long, dwindling,
    sunsets.
You bathe your limbs, you talk slowly; birds are all friendly?

V

Nightmare of future earth, again must I try
To build you. How can you be vaguely constructed,
Torment of dream,
Threatening to conquer: what are you like?
Shall it be thus? Two battleships for feet,
Two Eiffel Towers for legs, for your thin arms,
Two cranes that, either, lift ten thousand tons;
Your ribs long spans of bridges, your cold heart
Big Ben; your liver, clogged with bile, your guts, infirm,
Cluttered with refuse; your large belching stomach
Bulging with factories you have gulpingly swallowed;
All regulated by your clockwork heart?
But when at last I come to try your face,
I can see nothing, though your purple Siren
(So, Dream) can stroke it with arthritic hand.

You are held together by millions of wires and cables.
Could I alone cut one, one, the whole would fall apart.

VI

Now the moment is here to throw the gaunt gorilla
(Clutching my heart and making my dream)
Shivering with apish calls across the room.
He tumbles along the wainscot, becomes a shadow
Made by my lord, the Sun, the real
Redeemer, transmitter, transfuser, creator, giver, Receiver.

I rise at the open window; see real trees,
Real fields, real men, real dogs, real—Oh, the Charabanc,
Real; and there's the new, tall, factory chimney,
Real: and there, his cart-load real with bricks
The sawdust jerry-builder trolleys along the road,
Real. And how shall I finally murder the vaunting gorilla?
How can I ever succeed in protecting life, life, from the dream?

1924–5

THE EMPTY HOUSE

We were not wrong, believing that it cared;
When we had watched it gradually bared
Of furniture, I, going back alone,
Heard all its rafters moan.

It had become accustomed to our tread,
Our voices even, and the life we led.
I would wonder when I woke at night to hear
Its heart beating mysteriously near.

Or, when, arriving through the empty hall,
And feeling for the light, to catch the fall
Of shadows, where the ghostly rabble flies,
Frightened by human eyes.

(Ghosts are like instincts, little occupied
With time, and free of knowledge where they died.
They haunt, not having found the force to go,
Old houses they may know.)

Was it the mean desertion of a friend?
For all the time we plotted for the move
I thought the old house hearing: in the end
We nearly could not go because of love.

Toward the summer evening yesterday
What could I do but wander out that way?
And, looking at the house, what should I see,
From my own window staring back at me,

But my own image, definite and cold,
An early ghost, terrifyingly bold,
Haunting my former life, and making seem
My present body no more than a dream.

From that first moment many years ago
When first it did receive us, we by slow
Intent and movement modified the line
Of its design

So to receive our character and be
Friend to our various personality,
Gradually so to take us and to hold
Our furniture and form our outer mould,

That every angle slightly gave its place,
And even corners made a little space,
And open walls took shadow. But we are gone,
Except that I do haunt it still alone.

Unendingly imagination pries
Through every chink; the hand of memory tries
All darkened doors; the voice of habit falls
Along the empty walls.

And the strange dream lives on of those dead men
Who builded it together bit by bit,
And the forgotten people who since then
Were born in it, or lived and died in it.

c 1926

THE WINTER SOLSTICE

While they, those primitive men,
Were sacrificing all their fruits away,
Nevertheless the sun
Smouldered, and earlier sank each icy day,
Until at last his rays were so curtailed,
And they were driven back so far in dark,
That all began to think he might have failed.

In air they raised their gnarled and muscled arms,
Laying upon the troubled plain
Gigantic shadows, shrieking their alarms,
Invoking him, that only he remain,
Though, all the while, that old and regular sun
Gleamed on their frightened face,
Nor changed the purpose he had well begun.

At length when they discovered he was true,
That tortured season where he seems to go
Drowsing himself away in lemon blue
Under the earth, so low,
Became, no more a bleak lament for him,
But a large feast to glorify the rite,
The clean recapture of his former light.

We learned to flock together from the cold,
And mingle in the glow
Of rooms in which his captured gold
Provides ecstatic overflow . . .
While (memory can guess) plain-dutied Earth
Outside, and in the dark,
Is thrusting clumsy sap through stubborn clay,
And nearly, could one hark
Their crackling talk, one might discern the birth
Of leaves, and daffodils, and such as they.

1928

THE ONE, FAITHFUL . . .

How many many words may pass
Before one ever makes a friend
And all that conversation prove, alas,
However subtle, nothing in the end.

Searching I found and thought, "I will enrol
You slowly, peacefully among those of mine
Who can pass out beyond the initial toll
Of comradeship through necessary wine."

But, probing, I discovered, with what pain,
Wine more essential in the end than you,
And boon-companionship left me again
Less than I had been, with no more to do
Than drop pale hands towards their hips and keep
Friendship for speculation or for sleep.

We persons multiplied upon this earth
Meet hardly ever, or when we have found
Each other built congenial by our birth
Then we, just then, suspect the common ground
The voice, the way, the manner and the sound.

Friendship may be too difficult to win—
May end too quickly in a faint distrust,
Or may be found too sharply to begin
In its mere finding, a disgust.

So shall I turn to you my only friend
And going to you find you always there?
(I thought that) I return to you. I bend
My lips towards your eyes for what I miss
But just as we are sloping toward our kiss
I feel them moistened by your lonely tear.

BITTER SANCTUARY

I

She lives in the porter's room; the plush is nicotined.
Clients have left their photos there to perish.
She watches through green shutters those who press
To reach unconsciousness.

She licks her varnished thin magenta lips,
She picks her foretooth with a finger nail,
She pokes her head out to greet new clients, or
To leave them (to what torture) waiting at the door.

II

Heat has locked the heavy earth,
Given strength to every sound,
He, where his life still holds him to the ground,
In anæsthesia, groaning for re-birth,
Leans at the door.
From out the house there comes the dullest flutter;
A lackey; and thin giggling from behind that shutter.

III

His lost eyes lean to find and read the number.
Follows his knuckled rap, and hesitating curse.
He cannot wake himself; he may not slumber;
While on the long white wall across the road
Drives the thin outline of a dwindling hearse.

IV

Now the door opens wide.

He: "Is there room inside?"
She: "Are you past the bounds of pain?"
He: "May my body lie in vain
        Among the dreams I cannot keep!"
She: "Let him drink the cup of sleep."

V

Thin arms and ghostly hands; faint sky-blue eyes;
Long drooping lashes, lids like full-blown moons,
Clinging to any brink of floating skies:
What hope is there? What fear?—Unless to wake and see
Lingering flesh, or cold eternity.

O yet some face, half living, brings
Far gaze to him and croons:
She: "You're white. You are alone.
      Can you not approach my sphere?"
He: "I'm changing into stone."
She: "Would I were! Would / were!"
Then the white attendants fill the cup.

VI

In the morning through the world,
Watch the flunkeys bring the coffee;
Watch the shepherds on the downs,
Lords and ladies at their toilet,
Farmers, merchants, frothing towns.

But look how he, unfortunate, now fumbles
Through unknown chambers, unheedful stumbles.
Can he evade the overshadowing night?
Are there not somewhere chinks of braided light?

VII

How do they leave who once are in those rooms?
Some may be found, they say, deeply asleep
In ruined tombs.
Some in white beds, with faces round them. Some
Wander the world, and never find a home.

c 1931

BIBLIOGRAPHY

Monro collected what he considered to be his most satisfactory work in six small volumes: *Poems* (Elkin Mathews, July 1906), *Before Dawn (Poems and Impressions)* (Constable, July 1911), *Children of Love* (Poetry Bookshop, December 1914), *Strange Meetings* (Poetry Bookshop, April 1917), *Real Property* (Poetry Bookshop, March 1922) and *The Earth for Sale* (Chatto & Windus, May 1928). *Judas* (Samurai Press, early 1908, dated 1907) and *Trees* (Poetry Bookshop, December 1915, dated 1916) were published as independent volumes. Many more poems remained unpublished or appeared only in periodicals: some of these, together with the complete contents of the last four collections and a few poems from *Before Dawn*, were included in *The Collected Poems of Harold Monro* (Cobden-Sanderson, 1933). Monro also published four prose works, a play, an anthology and many articles and reviews.

There are as yet only two books about Monro: Joy Grant's critical and biographical study, *Harold Monro and the Poetry Bookshop* (1967), and Dominic Hibberd's biography, *Harold Monro: Poet of the New Age* (2001). See also the introductions to Monro's *Collected Poems* by F.S. Flint and T.S. Eliot (1933) and Ruth Tomalin (1970), and relevant chapters in Robert Ross, *The Georgian Revolt* (1967), and Samuel Hynes, *Edwardian Occasions* (1972).

NOTES

The note for each poem gives—where known—date and place of composition, followed where applicable by first publication in a periodical.

p.24 Impressions XI. Begun 28 July 1908, Gland, Switzerland. Monro was staying at a vegetarian sanatorium on Lake Geneva. On 2 August he lectured there (in French) on socialism to an audience of about 50 people.

p.25 Impressions X. 18 June 1908, Florence. One of the first poems written after Monro's Paris-Milan walk. Wilfred Owen, who came across a copy of *Before Dawn* in October 1911, quoted the first stanza in a January 1912 letter as a description of his own idleness (he was supposed to be working for exams at the time).

p.25 Impressions VIII. 15 August 1908, Gland. Monro, a keen vegetarian, had visited a London slaughterhouse in 1907.

p.26 Impressions I. This portrait of a hero-worker at sunrise is the introductory poem to the series of 30 'Impressions' in *Before Dawn;* it may have been written later than the others. Monro read it and other poems aloud to the Poetry Society in July 1910.

p.27 Go Now, Beloved. Early draft dated 21 June 1908, originally intended—improbably—as an 'Impression'. Monro was in Florence. Unlike most of the poems in *Before Dawn*, this is a confession of private feelings, referring to his first wife Dorothy and her current lover. Alida Klemantaski read the poem, among others, at the dinner where she first met Monro in 1913; he was upset, telling her afterwards that it was too personal to be read in public.

p.29 Two Visions. 9 January 1909, Garavan, near Menton. The introductory poem to *Before Dawn*. Based on two actual dreams and written next morning.

p.32 The Virgin. Probably early 1910, Monte Verita, Ascona, Switzerland. Monte Verita was one of the most influential free-thinking colonies in Europe. While Monro was there, the maverick psychoanalyst Otto Gross was preaching the gospel of sexual fulfilment. Gross's ideas later influenced D.H. Lawrence.

p.37 Paradise. 17 June 1910, Ascona. Monro had been engaged to Dorothy for a year ('One year in paradise'), before formal marriage had in his view helped to ruin their relationship. The values in the poem are typically Asconan.

p.39 Overheard on a Saltmarsh. *Rhythm*, November 1912; *Georgian Poetry* II (1915). The beads belonged to Vera Tchaikovsky, a Russian actress who apparently had an affair with Monro's friend, Arundel del Re.

p.40 London Interior. *Poetry Review*, December 1912. Probably describes 35 Devonshire Street just before its refurbishment as the Poetry Bookshop. Monro took the house in autumn 1912.

p.41 The Strange Companion. First drafted 1909–10, completed 1912–13. *Poetry and Drama*, June 1913. The 'companion' is alcohol. MS has amendments by Pound, who alters Monro's 'And both began together to advance' (l.5) and 'Yet he had a ceremonious way' (l.9) to 'And both of us advanced' and 'His way was ceremonious'. Monro ignored both suggestions but rewrote the lines. Pound chose this poem and the next three for his *Catholic Anthology* (November 1915), telling Monro he wanted work by poets who were 'looking straight at the thing, neither posing nor hugging an out of date illusion'.

p.43 Hearthstone. *Saturday Westminster Gazette*, 5 December 1914. The 'friend' may be Romney Green, the socialist furniture maker who fitted out the Bookshop.

p.44 Suburb. As readers have often noticed, parts of this poem foreshadow work by Eliot and Philip Larkin.

p.46 Milk for the Cat. *Georgian Poetry* II (1915). The popularity of this poem gave Monro the undeserved reputation of being a poet of animals: several reviewers of his *Collected Poems* expressed astonishment at the actual range of his subject-matter.

p.48 Youth in Arms. Four poems written in the early months of the Great War. Monro included the second and third in a Bookshop reading on 22 October 1914.

p.49 Soldier. *Saturday Westminster Gazette*, 7 November 1914.

p.49 Retreat. Refers to the British retreat from Mons in late August 1914. Newspapers, not yet subject to censorship, vividly reported the disaster. Men marched for days, sometimes hallucinating from weariness, keeping themselves going with snatches of song.

p.51 Carrion. All four 'Youth in Arms' poems show Monro's anxiety about his beloved friend Basil Watt. Like many other young men, Watt felt driven by conscience to join in the war effort. At first he opted for ambulance service, but he wanted to fight, despite Monro's warnings. In May 1915 he turned up at the shop in officer's uniform (see 'Lament in 1915'). The prophecy in 'Carrion' proved almost correct: Watt was killed on Hill 70 at Loos in September 1915, and his body was not found until long afterwards.

p.52 Lament in 1915 (B.H.W.). Late 1915, London. Basil Harry Watt: see note to preceding poem.

p.54 Trees. Earliest draft work in Monro's diary, 1 May 1915, a week after the death of Rupert Brooke. Most of the poem was written at 'Beake' (Beke), near Rayleigh, Essex, Monro's current weekend cottage. Probably finished after Watt's death. *English Review*, November 1915. In *Strange Meetings*, but also published as a hardback volume from the Bookshop, December 1915, in a limited edition printed by Arthur Sabin with woodcuts by James Guthrie.

p.60 Week-end. MS dated September 1915–April 1916. Written at Beake during weekends with Alida, who is shown as a close companion but not actually a sexual partner. *Georgian Poetry* III (1917). Presumably 'Week-end' is the source of the term 'weekend poetry', used sneeringly by critics after the war to describe Georgian work. 'Murry': the kettle was named after a slow-witted Bookshop assistant.

p.65 Strange Meetings. 1915–16, mostly written at Beake and its successor cottage, Chestnuts Farm, near Woodham Ferrers. Extracts in *English Review* and *Poetry* (USA), September 1916, and *Georgian Poetry* III (1917). Wilfred Owen certainly knew the poem: the title of his own 'Strange Meeting' must be a borrowing—perhaps meant to be recognised—from Monro (although it is also a quotation from Shelley). Owen had received useful advice from Monro in 1916 and had been interested in his poems since 1911 (see note on 'Impressions X').

p.73 Coronilla. Begun May 1913, Menton, where Monro was briefly on holiday. Completed November 1916. He is remembering his relationship with Dorothy—especially their final attempt to live together, at Menton in 1909. Coronilla: claw vetch, a southern plant with hooked tendrils. Paul Nash illustrated the poem with an engraving, later developed into a painting.

p.76 Solitude. Late 1916, Manchester. *Saturday Westminster Gazette*, 14 December 1916; *Georgian Poetry* III (1917). In October 1916 Alida bought a puppy to share her loneliness in London.

p.77 Aspidistra Street. MS dated December 1916, when Monro was in an army billet at 131 Queen (now Queensferry) Street, Newton Heath, Manchester.

p.78 Officers' Mess (1916). *Poetry*, February 1921. Monro never reprinted this poem, but it is in *Collected Poems* (1933). He became an officer in July 1916 and served only in England.

p.80 Real Property. First drafted in 1916 during army service, inspired by a letter from Alida about a vast cornfield she had just seen in Dorset. *To-Day*, July 1917; *Georgian Poetry* V (1922). Monro's legal studies in 1902 had included the laws of real property.

p.82 Fate. Draft dated 13 January 1920. *Poetry*, February 1922. The preceding poem had given Monro an idea for a series about humanity's true 'real property'. This and the next three poems are 'fragments' of this unfinished scheme: see Introduction.

p.85 The Garden. Final draft dated 29 January 1920. Part of humanity's 'real property' is the imagined possibility of perfection on earth, always just beyond reach. But Monro recognises that his own vision of the longed-for earthly paradise, which seems to include an ideal gay relationship, has to be prefaced by heavy drinking.

p.90 Introspection. *Poetry*, March 1920. Joy Grant first pointed out the similarity between this poem and parts of *The Waste Land.*

p.92 The Silent Pool. *New Republic* (USA), October 1921.

One draft entitled 'Blood'. Monro had probably seen the well-known Silent Pool at Albury, Surrey.

p. 95 Man Carrying Bale. Undated. *Georgian Poetry* IV (1919).

p.96 Unknown Country. First drafted 1913, probably completed *c* 1920. *The Dial*, March 1921; *Georgian Poetry* V (1922). Monro told Marsh the poem was 'almost too *Georgian* even for G.P.!' Pound protested in vain that old men could not be said to 'frolic' over their beer.

p.98 The Earth for Sale. MS marked 'Drafted 1922. Corrected and finished 1924'. *Chapbook*, October 1924; *English Journal* (USA), December 1925.

p.101 Holy Matrimony. MS dated 6 January 1924. Arundel del Re had been married a week earlier at a Roman Catholic church in Oxford; Monro had almost certainly attended the ceremony.

p.103 Living. MS dated 7 September 1924.

p.105 Midnight Lamentation. *Chapbook*, October 1924.

p.107 Dream Exhibition of a Final World. *Chapbook*, October 1925. A response to the British Empire Exhibition at Wembley, 1924. According to a contemporary guidebook, exhibits in the pavilions included mechanical copies of Niagara and at least one other famous waterfall, a 'realistic bit of forest', re-enactments of sea battles and an air raid, and a vast array of the latest machinery. Loudspeakers and wireless were prominently featured. The huge new stadium was used for military displays as well as sport and other spectacles. The poem's curious imagery seems cinematic: Monro may be thinking of recent films. The gorilla is a reminder of Darwinism: humanity is going back to the ape. The image of the crane occurs in several poems: London was busy repairing bomb damage, and there were cranes near the Bookshop.

p.111 The Empty House. Almost certainly describes 35 Devonshire Street just after Monro had vacated it in autumn 1926. Cp 'London Interior'. The building was reopened as Cecil House, a hostel for homeless women, in 1927, but it was destroyed in the Second World War.

p.113 The Winter Solstice. MS annotated, '27/4/28 I believe I may really have written a poem for the Ariel Poems. (Oh!) but we shall see tomorrow'. Monro was right: the poem was accepted by Faber and Gwyer for their Ariel Poems series and published in 1928 as a booklet with illustrations by David Jones. Eliot, who was a director of Faber's, asked Monro for a signed copy. Draft lines omitted from the final version hark back to sun-worship learned at Ascona: 'If we have lost our faith, let us return / To that enormous thought of him and know / That in his light we grow'.

p.114 The One, Faithful . . . Undated, presumably 1928 or later.

p.115 Bitter Sanctuary. *Criterion*, October 1931. Originally 'The Alcoholics'. Eliot commented that there was 'no one poem, no few poems, which I could point to and say: this will give you the essence of Monro; the nearest approach, and the dourest excruciation, is his last 'Bitter Sanctuary'. This one poem must at least demonstrate that Monro's vision of life was different from that of any of his contemporaries.'

INDEX OF TITLES

INDEX OF FIRST LINES